The C

Introducti

EmoT

2009 Edition

The Official

Introduction Guide to EmoTrance

2009 Edition

The Sidereus Foundation

Published by:

DragonRising Publishing

The StarFields Network Ltd

Compass House, 45 Gildredge Road

Eastbourne, East Sussex

United Kingdom

www.DragonRising.com

The Official Introduction Guide to EmoTrance

2009 Edition

ISBN: 978-1-873483-47-3

All Text & Images © The Sidereus Foundation 2007/2009

All Rights Reserved In All Media & Languages.

Published By:

DragonRising Publishing

The StarFields Network Ltd

Compass House, 45 Gildredge Road

Eastbourne, East Sussex, BN21 4RY

United Kingdom

Contact:

01323 700 123 (United Kingdom)

646 496 9857 (US + Canada)

0044 1323 700 123 (International)

www.DragonRising.com

For Further Information, Please Visit:

www.EmoTrance.com

Table of Contents

Table of Contents

Table of Contents

Table of Contents

Table of Contents

Table of Contents

Table of Contents

Table of Contents

Table of Contents

Welcome to EmoTrance 2009

We would like to welcome old and new friends alike to the 2009 edition of the Official Introduction Guide to EmoTrance.

EmoTrance celebrates its 7th birthday this year with over a thousand practitioners and trainers now all around the world, making a difference in their communities, helping people feel better and lead more hopeful, joyful and productive lives.

The wonderful clarity and simplicity of EmoTrance allows practitioners to go where all kinds of other "mind healing" approaches could not help but falter.

EmoTrance works directly with the energy system and the feedback of the physical body. There is no guesswork involved, and the basic, simple and very strict format of ASKING A PERSON WHERE IT HURTS, and dealing with that, and only that, is a huge relief to sufferers and practitioners alike.

Now, there is no need to go into the terrible details or the memories of what it was that caused the pain - the past only exists as data in our energy system, and it is relevant only in the pain which it causes right here, right now, TODAY.

We don't need to dwell on the past and we don't need to re-live the past. We don't need to think about it, ask, "Why oh why?" or even share with another soul what it was that caused the pain.

EmoTrance is ONLY about right here and now.

If there is emotional pain present, we can heal it via the energy system - simply, quickly, and beautifully.

As such, EmoTrance is entirely unique amongst therapy forms. No speech is needed, we work only with the body sensations and that means that even the oldest injuries, sustained long, long before there was the power of speech or conscious thought can be healed with EmoTrance.

Another wonderful and quite unique advantage lies in the fact that an EmoTrance practitioner does not have to study for ages, learn about all kinds of problems and their names, learn about all kinds of channels or parts of the energy body - it is completely unnecessary to the EmoTrance process, and some even hold it to be counter-productive to start naming the energy system.

The fact is that every person's energy system is unique, and the energy bodies of those who really need help with "emotional problems" are much more unique than the average.

Traumatic and painful events have shaped and re-shaped the energy system over time, and maps drawn on some imaginary perfection simply will not do in a territory that might look like a country after a long war, with bridges torn and broken, and no roads leading from there to here.

For the client, EmoTrance is a HUGE relief. For once, the practitioner does not presume to know better, or to know everything. The practitioner cannot know - so they must ask.

We call this the "client-practitioner dance" which allows both the client and the practitioner to discover together how things are, and what must be done by both working together as a team of equals to bring back the Even Flow, when pain has ceased, energy flows again, and a person experiences wonderful peace, joy, and mental and emotional clarity.

It is true that the client-practitioner dance is also a huge relief for the practitioner, who doesn't have to be some kind of super being with the knowledge of the ages at the ready to simply ASSIST ANOTHER HUMAN BEING to be healed of their pain, and to find joy and hope again.

Time and time again we have seen that people LOVE to help others - but they don't really know what to do, or how to help, or how to let that compassion and desire for "making right what once went wrong" to become a powerful ally in really healing parts of a human being that have been neglected so bitterly, by so many, and for so long.

EmoTrance being so structural, so simple and so NATURAL to human beings means that there are no barriers of age, ability, society, religion or education that would exclude a person from learning EmoTrance, and using it to good effect right away with those who are sad, and suffering from the types of pain that no doctor can help them with.

This makes EmoTrance the perfect first aid device for emotional suffering right at the forefront and in the most demanding and difficult of circumstances.

A simple nurse in a field hospital anywhere in the world can learn EmoTrance in less than an hour; so can an aid worker. It doesn't stop there, however. The inmates of a hospital or a refugee camp can learn it too, and will understand it just as quickly as those who are more educated.

In fact, it has been our observation that simple people find EmoTrance simple to learn; even little children as young as three years old can learn EmoTrance, and have even been observed to transmit this knowledge to another child who was crying.

EmoTrance is a truly extraordinary form of healing painful emotions from the past.

As if that wasn't good enough, there is a whole other side to EmoTrance, for it isn't "just" a therapy.

The presuppositions of EmoTrance open the door to having completely different experiences of the world.

EmoTrance doesn't just take old pain away and brings peace, it goes much further than that.

Amazingly, once the energy system is healed of a major injury, and there is a better, faster flow of energy through the energy body, people begin to come to life and experience all sorts of positive emotions and sensations - it is literally, the other side of peace.

And on the other side of peace, there lies excitement, feeling alive, feeling vibrant, feeling full of energy, the mind becoming clear and active, and the body waking up as well.

EmoTrance is exciting in that way.

Even people who had long given up on feeling good, or bright or young again, find a significant change in their outlook and what they might hope to experience in the future.

With the concept of Energy Nutrition, deliberately soaking up beneficial energies and running them through our systems, comes a whole new world of brand new experiences; feelings that were never felt before, and states of excitement and aliveness that may have been previously entirely unknown to a person.

People feel feelings they have never felt before.

EmoTrance is extremely enriching; and as the ability to feel energy in one's body has nothing to do with youth or fitness, even people who are old, or sick, can gain good feelings AT WILL through the practise of EmoTrance.

All it takes is a sunrise, a beautiful flower or a beautiful person, or any part of nature to become energized in a very specific and unusual way - and as long as a person can remember to do that, they will ALWAYS have wondrous moments in every single day.

It is this, in the end, that makes EmoTrance truly unique and so delightful - EmoTrance brings back hope, and not just hope, but it delivers.

For an EmoTrance user with a little bit of experience, the world becomes a totally different place.

Unpleasant experiences and emotions are overcome very quickly; and whether or not one would like to experience joy is entirely in your hands, at your decision.

People's emotion driven behaviours make much more sense, as do their strange disturbed thinking patterns. It is much, much easier to remain calm and compassionate, because it becomes so obvious that people are not "bad" or "out to get you", they are just in pain and reacting as anyone would, who would be in pain the same.

EmoTrancers develop a totally different viewpoint on addictions of all kinds, and because emotions no longer frighten them, find that they begin to become more adventurous once more. Many revise what they thought they could or could not achieve in this lifetime; and many others find they have so much more energy, they can achieve much more than they ever thought possible.

It is our supposition that EmoTrance works as well as it does, and that it has all these beneficial side effects with absolutely none of the usual problems you would find with therapies or healing modalities, because it is based on a correct theory and correct assessment of "how things really are".

Yes, there are "invisible" layers of information and energy everywhere.

Yes, we do have an energy body and it needs us to become aware of it, to feed it right, treat it right, or else we'll never be happy, no matter how well we eat or how rich we become.

Yes, we have a simple method now to understand the energy body and to assist it and to heal it - and it works like a charm!

And finally - YES, the Creative Order who made us the way we are gave us emotions not so that we should suffer, but in the contrary, that we should suffer as little as possible and the rest of the time, have WONDERFUL and delightful feelings, sensations and experiences in the world.

EmoTrance is a wonderful modality. Take it for a test drive. Make it your own. You will find that as time goes by and you re-learn how to use your own mind and energy system the way it was designed to be used in the first place, you too will come to appreciate the beauty, power, freedom but most of all, the JOY EmoTrance can help you put right into your own life.

Welcome to the wonderful world of EmoTrance!

The EmoTrance Primer

Introduction To The EmoTrance Primer

by Dr Silvia Hartmann, Creator, EmoTrance

All the original research and all the books on EmoTrance are in the English language and were originally designed for natural English speakers.

Through the medium of the Internet, EmoTrance was world wide from the start and soon enough, there arose the problem of translation.

As EmoTrance contains a number of unique concepts, which are reflected in the words that are being used, and which are so important as intention influences the energy flow absolutely, and the wrong words spoken, the wrong thoughts thought will have a strong impact on how well EmoTrance will work, and how quickly, The EmoTrance Primer was created.

The purpose of The EmoTrance Primer is to have a single document which simply and directly transmits the core ideas and practices of EmoTrance to every human being, regardless of how formally educated they may be.

Further, The EmoTrance Primer in its very simple language was designed in consultation with a number of non-English speakers so that it is easy to translate, and errors and misunderstandings become a thing of the past.

With its limitless applications for every aspect of human life and endeavour, there is a great reservoir of techniques and approaches in the EmoTrance system.

The very core of EmoTrance, however, is available to all human beings and it is from this core that all the other myriad of applications and possibilities arise.

The EmoTrance Primer was created for use in the field, in the many arenas where humans need help around the world, so that people can help other people, without having to spend much money or study which is often entirely inaccessible in the very places where this help is needed the most.

But even for the most advanced, knowledgeable and experienced energy workers amongst us, The EmoTrance Primer is an opportunity to go back to the basics and to know and understand that this is what EmoTrance is about, and never to lose this, no matter how wondrous or exciting the advanced applications for the 1st World users & researchers may become.

Dr Silvia Hartmann
Creator, EmoTrance
October 2007

The EmoTrance Primer

1. **Emotions are very important.**

   Emotions affect our body and can make us sick.

   Emotions affect our mind and can make us go crazy.

   Emotions affect our thoughts and actions, every day.

   Emotions affect our health and our relationships, every day.

2. **People make decisions based not on logic, but on emotions.**

   - Our human world is created by EMOTION and runs on EMOTION.

   - Happy people don't lie, cheat and steal.

   - Happy people don't hurt one another.

   - Happy people don't go to war.

3. **EmoTrance helps people feel better.**

   - EmoTrance transforms emotions.

   - That is what EmoTrance does.

4. **Emotions are feelings that have no physical cause.**

   - People say, "My heart is breaking."

   - There is pain in their chest, and they can hardly breathe.

   - If you look at their chest, you see nothing.

   - There is no knife in their chest; nothing is wrong with their body. But they can feel the pain.

5. People have a physical body.

- The physical body has a heart.

- The physical body has a head.

- The physical body has hands, a stomach, veins with blood, many organs.

- When the physical body is injured, people experience physical pain.

- Physical pain tells us when something is wrong with the physical body.

- When we step on a sharp stone with our foot, it is our foot that hurts.

- The physical pain tells us where the injury is located in the physical body.

6. People have an energy body.

- The energy body too has a heart, a head, a stomach, many veins, and many organs.

- It is all made out of energy.

- When the energy body is injured, people experience emotional pain.

- Emotions tell us when something is wrong with the energy body.

- When we have emotional pain and feel it in the heart, it is the energy heart that is injured.

- If we feel the emotion in the stomach, it is the energy stomach that is injured.

- The emotional pain tells us where the injury is located in the energy body.

7. **You can't see the energy body.**

   - But you can feel the energy body.

8. **When the energy body is well, people feel happy.**

   - They have lots of energy.
   - They smile. They eat well and sleep well.
   - They are friendly to other people.
   - When the energy body is not well, people feel bad.
   - They are sad, or angry.
   - They don't smile. They don't feel right.
   - They get angry and annoyed with other people.

9. **The energy body is not hurt by sticks and stones.**

   - The energy body is hurt only by energy.
   - The energy body cannot be healed with knives and operations.
   - The energy body is healed only by energy.

10. **We have healing hands made from energy.**

    - The energy hands are a part of everyone's energy body.
    - We have an energy mind that understands all about energy and the energy body.
    - The energy mind is a part of everyone's energy body.
    - Our thinking mind can learn to tell the energy hands to start healing the energy body.
    - The energy hands, guided by the energy mind, will know what to do.

11. A person is...

- **... very sad.**
    - We ask: "Where do you feel this in your body?"
    - We say: "Show me with your hands."
    - Now we know exactly where the problem is, even though we cannot see the energy body.

- **... very angry.**
    - We ask: "Where do you feel this in your body?"
    - We say: "Show me with your hands."
    - Now we know exactly where the problem is, even though we cannot see the energy body.

- **... very afraid.**
    - We ask: "Where do you feel this in your body?"
    - We say: "Show me with your hands."
    - Now we know exactly where the problem is, even though we cannot see the energy body.

12. There is no sadness or fear or anger in a person's energy body.

- We say, "It is only an energy."
- The energy body is broken and the sadness and fear and anger are the calls for help from the energy body.
- It is the same as the physical body calls for help with pain.

13. We repair the energy body.

- When the energy body is repaired, the emotions are different.

- Instead of sad and fear and anger, there will be happiness and peace and joy.

14. You know that the energy body has been repaired when there is happiness and peace and joy.

We call this the Even Flow.

To bring back the Even Flow in the energy body is the purpose of EmoTrance.

15. We breathe in with our physical body, we take the goodness from the air, and breathe out what we don't need.

- We eat with our physical body, we take the goodness from the food and water, and let go of what we don't need.

- The energy body needs to take in energy.

- The energy needs to run through the energy body.

- The energy body takes out what it needs.

- It lets go of the rest.

- We say, "The energy needs to flow in, through, and out."

16. In our physical body, blood must flow everywhere.

- In our energy body, energy must flow everywhere.

- When the energy does not flow, we feel bad.

17. We say: "Energy is like water."

- When energy flows freely, it is like fresh, clear water and it feels good.

- When there is a blockage, you feel pressure building up.

- The energy flows slowly like thick, dense water.

- If the pressure builds up more, the energy becomes harder and harder until it starts to hurt.

- Some people start to cry.

- Some people get very angry.

- Some people become afraid.

- Some people get silent and depressed.

- But it is always only energy.

18. In EmoTrance, we make the energy flow freely again.

- We ask, "Where does this energy need to go?"

- We say to our energy mind and our healing energy hands: "Soften and flow!"

- The energy mind understands what that means and the healing energy hands help make that happen.

19. In the energy body there are many natural channels.

- Energy flows freely through those channels in, through, and out.

- When the energy flow is blocked, we experience painful emotions.

- We find the right channels and we help the energy flow with our healing hands.

20. We do not need to know about the channels.

- We ask, "Where does this need to go?"

- We say, "Soften and flow."

- We help the energy move through the right channels all the way out of the energy body.

- When we do this, we start to feel much better.

21. When one person helps another person with EmoTrance, we say:

- "I am going to help move the energy from the outside, and you help move the energy from the inside."

- Both people must want the energy to flow freely again.

- Both people say, "Soften and flow!"

- Both people want the Even Flow to be restored.

- Then their healing hands and energy minds will go to work and make it happen.

22. Our thoughts have an effect on energy.

- We can build walls and shields made of energy around our energy bodies.

- We do this to keep energy out that hurts.

- Energy only hurts when there is an injury in the energy body.

- This is like salt only hurts when there is an injury in the skin.

- We must repair the injury first and then there is no need for walls and shields.

23. Our physical body needs lots of food and water to stay healthy.

- Our energy body needs lots of different kinds of energy to stay healthy.
- Our energy body needs energy from nature, and from other people.

24. Walls and shields keep energy out and that makes our energy body weak.

- When our energy body is weak and hungry, we feel sad, lonely, angry, afraid and depressed.

25. We ask, "Where do you feel this energy in your body?"

- Someone says, "I don't feel anything at all."
- We say, "There is a shield. The energy cannot come into your body. That is why you don't feel it."
- We ask, "Where is this shield? Show me with your hands."
- Now we know where the shield is.

26. The shield is made of energy.

- Our thoughts can change things made from energy.
- We say, "Make a very small hole in the shield and let a little bit of energy come in."
- We say, "Where do you feel this in your body? Show me with your hands."
- Now we know where the injury is and why there is a shield or a wall.
- We heal the injury.
- Now we don't need the shield anymore.

- The energy comes in, goes through and out.
- The energy body is no longer hungry.
- The person feels much better.

27. A person has bad memories of the past.

- There are many bad memories.
- We do not talk about the bad memories or the past.
- We ask, "Where are you in pain today? Show me with your hands."
- We heal the energy body.
- The person is no longer in pain today.

28. A person has been in a war.

- There were many terrible experiences.
- We do not have to talk about the many terrible experiences.
- We ask, "Where does it hurt the most? Show me with your hands."
- We heal the energy body.
- The person remembers everything that happened, but it doesn't hurt any more.

29. A person has been attacked.

- They are very angry.
- We do not have to talk about not being angry.
- We ask, "Where do you feel that anger in your body? Show me with your hands."
- We heal the energy body.

- The person remembers everything but they are not angry any longer.

30. A person's child has died.

- They are very sad and very angry. They are in pain.

- We do not have to talk about their sad and angry.

- We ask, "Where do you feel the pain? Show me with your hands."

- We heal the energy body.

- The person remembers everything but they are no longer in pain.

- The person remembers the beauty of their child, and the love of their child.

31. A person was in an accident.

- They had an operation to repair the physical body.

- Their body looks healed but they still feel pain.

- Doctors tell them, "There is nothing wrong with you."

- We ask, "Where do you feel this pain in your body? Show me with your hands."

- We heal the energy body.

- Now the whole person is healed and the pain is gone.

32. A person says, "I have these terrible thoughts."

- We say, "Emotional pain causes terrible thoughts. Where do you feel the pain in your body? Show me with your hands."

- We heal the energy body. The person is not in pain any longer and the thoughts are clear and calm.

33. A person has a terrible illness.

- They say, "Heal me of this illness in my body!"

- We say, "We only heal emotional pain, not illness in the body. How do you feel about your illness?"

- The person says, "I am very afraid all the time."

- We say, "Would it help you not to be very afraid all the time?"

- The person says, "Yes."

- We say, "Where do you feel that very afraid in your body? Show me with your hands."

- We heal the energy body.

- We do not heal the illness.

- The person is still ill but they are not so very afraid all the time any more.

- We have helped this person.

34. People say, "You have to be a great healer to heal the energy body."

- We say, "Everybody has an energy body. Everyone has healing hands and everyone has an energy mind. Everyone who has ever felt an emotion can learn to do EmoTrance."

35. People say, "You have to study many books for many years to heal the energy body."

- We say, "Ask the person where it hurts. Ask them to show you with their hands. Ask them where the energy needs to go. Help them make it flow again. It is easy."

36. People say, "I have had this terrible problem for many years. It will take as many years to heal it."

- We say, "Energy flows quickly. Energy is very fast. It won't take as many years to heal the terrible problem because the terrible problem is only energy now."

37. People say, "I need to keep my problem because it is important that I should suffer."

- We say, "It is only energy. We restore the Even Flow. We repair what was broken."

38. People say, "Why wasn't I told this before?"

- We say, "We don't know. But now EmoTrance is here and now we can heal the energy body so we feel happiness instead of pain."

39. EmoTrance works ONLY with energy.

- EmoTrance does not heal the physical body.

- EmoTrance heals the energy body.

- To heal the energy body is very important.

- There are too few people who help heal the energy body.

- A person with a sick energy body might not look sick, but their lives are not good lives.

40. **It is very important for people to feel happiness and peace and joy.**

   - If the energy body is working well, everything in life becomes easier.

   - We can work better.

   - We can think better.

   - We can heal faster.

   - We can be better parents, friends, and we can help other people.

41. **To be an EmoTrance practitioner means to help people find happiness and peace and joy where there was pain.**

   - It is a very powerful experience.

42. **EmoTrance can help you find happiness and peace and joy in your life.**

43. **The Heart Healing Prayer**

I put my healing hands
On my heart of energy
To heal what once was broken
To make right what once went wrong
To soften and to flow
To restore the Even Flow
So that my heart of energy
can once again
shine like the sun.

44. You can do EmoTrance for yourself.

- EmoTrance is easy to learn.

- EmoTrance is natural.

- All human beings can learn to do EmoTrance.

- Children can learn to do EmoTrance.

45. Notice when you feel emotions in your body.

- Where do you feel your fear, your anger, your sadness?

- Show yourself with your hands.

- Pay attention every day to the emotions in your body.

46. Use your healing hands of energy.

- Put your healing hands of energy on your body where the pain is. Ask, "Where does this need to go?"

- Say, "Soften and flow!"

- Pay attention to where the energy wants to go.

- Help it flow all the way through and out of your body.

- The more you do EmoTrance, the easier it becomes.

47. Let more energy come into your energy body.

- Take a moment each day to draw the energy of the sun in, through and out.

- Let the energy of many things flow into you.

- Flowers, animals, stones, water, the earth, the sky, trees all have wonderful life energy.

- People, music, works of art, angels are different forms of energy that feel good too.

48. Let energy burdens flow away.

- Ask, "Is my energy body carrying any burdens? Where do I feel this in my body?" Say, "These burdens are only an energy! Where do they need to go? Soften and Flow!"

- When the burdens have gone, you will feel much better.

49. Energy must always flow.

- Sometimes people try to hold on to energy in their energy body.

- This is very unhealthy.

- Ask, "Am I holding on to old energy? Where do I feel this in my body?" Say, "This is only an energy. Energy must flow. Where does it need to go? Soften and Flow!"

- When the energy flows again, you will feel much better.

50. When energy flows freely in the body, the emotions are wonderful.

- People discover good feelings they have never felt before.

- The body feels stronger, the mind thinks more clearly and the emotions are bright and wonderful.

- We call this the Energized End State.

51. EmoTrance is very useful.

- You can use it anywhere because no-one can see it.

- You can use EmoTrance to flow away fear, anger and sadness as soon as it comes to you.

- You can use it to heal the past.

- You can use EmoTrance to have a better life today.

- You can use EmoTrance to fill yourself with beautiful energy any time you want - and it is all free!

- Even for a beginner, EmoTrance makes a big difference.

- With practise, EmoTrance gets better, and better!

Learn more about EmoTrance.

Find your local practitioners, trainers and events at:

www.EmoTrance.com

Please Feel Free To Translate & Distribute

The EmoTrance Primer

by Dr Silvia Hartmann

This is simple but important knowledge

and it can help people lead better lives.

EmoTrance Introductions

Here you can find some examples of introductions to EmoTrance by different people, using different words and different examples.

EmoTrance is entirely free of dogma and it is highly personal; each person who learns EmoTrance makes it their own and OWNS IT absolutely from the moment they first understood how it works.

This is also the case for the EmoTrance practitioners and trainers. With so many potential applications and literally infinite possibilities for using and teaching EmoTrance around the world and to so many different groups of people, the practitioners and trainers go where their own hearts lead them.

Why EmoTrance Is Simply The Best!

by Nicola Quinn, EmoTrance Co-Developer

Energy Healing Made Simple

Quite simply EmoTrance is the easiest energy healing modality in the world today and that in my view makes it the best. Once learned it is always there and because of its superb simplicity you can rely on it at a moment's notice. In fact the more you do it, the more spontaneously it occurs, you just become aware of energy moving through you.

Where do you feel that in your body?

Show me with your hands.

Soften and Flow.

It's only an energy!

And that is all you need to remember. What could be easier.

The simplicity of EmoTrance is superb. It's so easy you can teach it to a child, in fact most children do it quite naturally!

EmoTrance deals beautifully with:

- Relationship and love pain
- Fear and anxiety stress
- Stuck pain including past hurts
- Shields that prevent us from experiencing the sometimes delightful messiness that is life itself!

Back to Nature

Our bodies naturally want to do EmoTrance, they want to move energy, that's how they are made and once natural flows are again established there is nothing to be afraid of, nothing that can hurt you or affect you as it did before. Once you have regained Even Flow you are quite literally back in tune with nature and your body, your emotions, your thoughts and indeed your whole life are simply transformed as they fall back into alignment with the rhythms of the universe.

Heal Relationship Pain with EmoTrance

Healing love pain is one of the easiest things to do with EmoTrance and is one of the first ways a lot of people get to hear about it.

In fact that was how EmoTrance came into being! I was having a telephone conversation with my friend Silvia Hartmann and commented on the pain I was feeling after someone close to me had said something nasty, I was really suffering that morning, as if I had been punched in the stomach, and it was the first time I heard Silvia Hartmann say, "Where do you feel that in your body?" and the rest, as they say, is history!

We spent several hours after that hurling insults and compliments down the phone at each other until we made each of the energies run really cleanly through ourselves and ended up laughing wildly.

Here is how I helped a lady over the phone with her relationship pain in moments.

Relationship Pain Healed in Seconds!

A lady phoned me the other day about EmoTrance. She wanted to know more about it after reading an article in a magazine about relationships which had mentioned the technique and she was desperate to know what it was and how many sessions she would need as she had been suffering for so long.

Now normally I would have directed her to the website for more information and recommended a practitioner but on this occasion I asked her what the problem was and she said she had this terrible feeling since she found out her husband was having an affair and then left her two years ago which she just could not get rid of, whatever she did, it was there day and night despite her best efforts to get on with her life.

She couldn't put her finger on what it was, anger, guilt, sadness or the sheer terror of being on her own now and raising 3 small children.

I asked her where she felt it in her body and told her to put her hands there and she instantly said, my chest, like an enormous weight which just won't lift and some days feel it is going to squash the life out of me.

I told her that the feeling was only an energy as there obviously wasn't a heavy weight on her chest at this moment and that because it is only energy she can move it with her intention.

I asked her where she thought the energy might like to go and within moments she said, Oh my god! It's gone up and out the top of my head!

I then asked her how her chest felt now and she was astonished and said absolutely fine. I told her to think about her husband and she said she still felt nothing, it was gone, and there was such relief in her voice as she started to laugh.

Oh my god that's amazing, I have my life back, thank you so much! were the last words I heard from her as she put the phone down.

Now I know EmoTrance is quick but that conversation was about two minutes long, absolute maximum, and with a woman who had had no experience of energy therapies in her life before.

I think we were both equally astonished at the end of that call and I just shook my head and smiled at the wonder of this extraordinary technique and how much suffering can be relieved so simply and quickly.

EmoTrance and Better Sex

The excellent thing about EmoTrance is that as you become more aware of physical sensations you become far more responsive which can enhance your sex life immeasurably.

Just try this simple exercise:

Learning To Follow With Intention

1. Touch or have another touch you lightly with one fingertip on the arm or some other part of your body.

2. Have them lightly massage or tap the area.

3. Follow the touch as it travels through your system with your intention.

4. Repeat on different parts of your body until such touches flow instantly and smoothly.

Here is how I helped a friend achieve a better sex life with EmoTrance.

A while back a friend called round and after a while chatting she started moaning about sex not being as good as it used to be and that she had got into a bit of a spiral of not wanting it so much as her partner was now getting all frustrated and bitchy with her which of course was making her want it even less.

I asked her what the problem was and she said she wasn't having orgasms anymore, she was reaching a certain point of fairly intense sensations but was not quite getting there and the whole effort involved just didn't seem worth it.

When I asked her what would have to happen next to achieve orgasm she thought for a moment and said the feeling would need to spread upwards in her body which immediately made me think of a time, way before EmoTrance even had a name and I was still referring to it as the Gorgeous Pattern, when I had used the idea of moving energy to overcome a serious attack of feet tickling I was being subjected to.

I have always had extremely ticklish feet but instead of writhing around trying to get away I concentrated on pulling the feeling up my legs, thinking all the time, it's only an energy, let it flow where it wants to go. I found the feeling changed from an intense overwhelming sensation to a most pleasurable tingling as the energy flowed up my legs.

So I told my friend to take off her shoes and started gently tickling her feet getting her to consciously pull the feelings upwards until she could do it without wriggling and screaming wildly.

I wasn't sure this was going to be the answer to her problem but it's a pretty neat thing to be able to do anyway.

I hadn't heard from her for a while and thought nothing more of it until she phoned yesterday apologising for not being in touch sooner saying that she had been fairly busy, namely being all over her man. She now couldn't get enough of him and said that the technique had been extremely successful giving her the most powerful, satisfying orgasms she has ever had.

She also said that she had taught her partner the technique and he had used it to delay ejaculation which had also added enormous pleasure to the whole proceedings!

When I put the phone down I must admit I had to EmoTrance through a rather large amount of envy ...

Martial Arts and EmoTrance - Let That Chi Flow!

Not only does EmoTrance deal with emotional pain but it also re-establishes even flow within the energy system allowing more control over the flow of chi, ch'i, ki, qi or whatever your pet name for the life force energy may be!

Once your energy channels are open and flowing smoothly martial arts practices become a lot easier and cleaner, balance is easier to maintain and an inner centredness is achieved in seconds.

EmoTrance is a perfect adjunct to Tai chi, Aikido, Karate, Chi gung, Kung fu, Jujitsu, Kendo, Judo, Tae kwon do and improves performance, strength, focus and awareness.

Energy Nutrition Helps Overcome Cravings and Addictions

We all know how important it is to get enough vitamins and minerals to maintain heath and we know that what we eat, whether good or bad, quite quickly shows its effects on our bodies. A little abuse, too much alcohol and junk food soon manifests as low energy, restlessness, bad skin and hair, to name but a few side effects but with EmoTrance the idea of nutrition goes much, much further.

Imagine what it would be like to literally suck the energy out of anything, really absorb and metabolise it! Many people have already used EmoTrance to overcome cravings and addictions in this way. The possibilities are endless and it is great fun finding new ways to use this too.

EmoTrance and Children - For Bullying, Confidence and Fears

EmoTrance should be taught in every school! Children love EmoTrance and if you make a game of it they love it even more.

It is the perfect way to help children learn to cope with not only their emotions but any bad things other children may say to them. Once they learn to EmoTrance hurtful things through and out and actually get energised by them they have the perfect tool to help combat bullying. It does not turn them into heartless tough little things but increases their breadth of experience and gives them confidence.

Here is a wonderful story about how Silvia Hartmann helped a boy with Asperger's overcome many fears using EmoTrance.

Asperger's Boy Fears Of Other Children

I did an EmoTrance session with an Asperger's diagnosed 12 year old boy this morning relating to fear of being noticed and being looked at because he had to attend a public concert at a local school with his group from the special unit and had a lot of fear about it.

I explained about feelings being stuck energy that needs to leave somewhere and he accepted this readily and without argument. It took a little while to have him locate the physical sensations relating to the fears but once he had found the first one, it all went astonishingly smoothly and easily from there.

First there was fear of being noticed by the other children, in his stomach, which moved up and came out through his mouth. He was much calmer after that.

Then, there was a fear of being looked at directly, in his head. This moved all around and came out through his skin.

Next was fear of what they would say to him - comments about his looks, about being stupid. Once he had the hang of it, he actually started to giggle when I told him sternly that he was a total idiot and useless as well to test that the channels for that were running cleanly now.

Then he mentioned another fear, namely that of his parents being upset when the staff told them afterwards about him "having had a bad day", producing looks and demeanour of disappointment in the parents, and silence. This was in his chest and took the longest to move, half went up and out of the top of his head, the other down his back.

I then offered him to do "one on me" - don't know why, just happened - and he readily yelled some abuse at me which he truly enjoyed and also, was paying intense attention to me and fascinated with how it moved around and out for **me**. For whatever reason I cannot fathom, I asked him to tell me that "You have failed, I knew you would! I knew it all along!"

It was fascinating how this boy who is normally very, very reserved and expressionless really got into that and shouted it at me, flat out, with the intensity of an Oscar winning actor and with full meaning AND eye contact (he doesn't normally give any eye contact at all).

When he did, it really did something extraordinary to my systems, a huge effect and sensation that led to me saying to him that I understood now that it's not the winning or failing, but having had the guts to TRY in the first place that takes the medal.

I'm really not sure what happened there or why I did that, if it was for him or for me or for both of us but it certainly wasn't like any therapy session I've ever conducted or experienced, ever.

The practical outcome was also very interesting. In a session after the concert had happened he told me that he hadn't "freak out" beforehand and had looked forward to the public performance. He told me he even had noticed the unusual thought that he wanted to respond to someone who said something to him.

He also at one point during the performance at the school, got a pen out and wrote his own name on his arm, upside down so that one could read it if one was looking at him, and stated that he "had no idea why he did it and only noticed after he had done it".

I suggested the idea that there was a part of him that really wanted people to know his name and who he was, and this other part that was still traumatised and needing to hide away after having been bullied and hurt at his previous school and he agreed that this was the most likely reason for the "name writing". He was very accepting of it all, very open, perfectly happy to talk to me about it - that in and of itself is totally unheard of with this boy, such a breakthrough, it's extraordinary.

It is the weirdest thing. I've known this boy for quite a while and today it was like I've found myself in a totally different country with him, that wasn't therapy or anything like that, something different altogether - I just don't know quite how to describe it. But it was good, and I just can't think of him as a client or a child at all now but I'm thinking of him as a fellow person, just equal in some way - very strange but very satisfying indeed.

Is EmoTrance The Same As EFT?

In a word, No! With EmoTrance you do not need to think about how you are feeling or formulate an opening statement, or tap, or measure how bad you are feeling. You simply locate where the discomfort or pain is in your body and work from there, no guessing, or wondering if you are on the right track. EmoTrance bypasses the brain and the endless guessing and deals directly with the feedback from our bodies. Stuck energy feels bad. Move it out of your body and you feel better. Simple.

EmoTrance is content free, you don't need to know what caused the pain, you don't need to create any opening statements, you don't need to tap, you just have to know where it is, show me with your hands, soften and flow, and it is gone!

Is EmoTrance Safe?

EmoTrance is completely safe and ecologically sound, there are no repercussions, backlashes, regressions to past behaviours. Through relentless testing by thousands worldwide we know this to be true.

EmoTrance is not only safe but an absolute joy to work with, it lifts and brightens the spirit, that's part of its design, you cannot fail to feel better, a fabulous by product of this simple but profound technique.

And that's because EmoTrance does not just stop at the cessation of pain, it goes much, much further than that. The energised end state leaves you tingling, and giggling, lighter and brighter than you have ever felt before. In fact it's not really EmoTrance unless you feel like that at the end of a session!

But more than all of this EmoTrance is a way of life, a way of renewing our contact with our environment and the people around us.

How Can I Learn EmoTrance?

You can start by reading the excellent Oceans of Energy - The Patterns and Techniques of EmoTrance, Vol. 1 by Silvia Hartmann or you can enrol on the EmoTrance Online Distance Training Course which is not only a certification training for practitioners but is also a superb introduction to EmoTrance itself and is used by many to get a really deep understanding of how EmoTrance works. And if you do the online training you get me to support you as tutor every step of the way!

You can also attend one of the many Live EmoTrance Trainings which incorporate an introductory day where you can go along and experience EmoTrance with a fully qualified trainer. And there are also many hundreds of Certified EmoTrance Practitioners worldwide who would be happy to give you an individual session, in person or on the telephone.

I hope this little introduction will whet your appetite and spur you on to investigate further the wonderful world of EmoTrance and all its many applications and possibilities to enrich your life and help you navigate the vast Oceans of Energy with ease and delight!

Nicola Quinn, EmoTrance Co-Creator, 2005

What Is EmoTrance?

By Alex Kent

I was recently asked by an EmoTrance Trainer to define EmoTrance for a magazine article for therapists in no more than 200 words. After a couple of hours of trying to include such a broad set of systems and techniques as EmoTrance, in such a short word count, I came up with the following...

"EmoTrance is a set of simple yet profound tools and techniques pioneered by Dr Silvia Hartmann, PhD and Nicola Quinn for working with the human energetic emotional systems. EmoTrance throws away the old maps, rituals and eliminates guesswork by asking the client to show them literally where the energetic emotional disturbance takes place.

By working with the natural kinaesthetic feedback mechanisms of the human body, the treatment is tailor made to the client who is not required to describe what caused the emotional disturbance in the first place. However, once the EmoTrance session has concluded the client normally tells you what their history was because it doesn't hurt or bother them anymore!

EmoTrance has been skilfully designed to be simple, effective, natural, gentle and respectful to the client, their history and beliefs. Working with EmoTrance gives you the perfect complimentary technique to your existing knowledge and qualifications, as well as giving you the ability to take yourself and others into new realms of happiness."

Whilst the trainer was most satisfied by this, I reflected that a newbie might be left thinking that the world of EmoTrance was all about fixing and patching, instead of flying and soaring! In essence, a description for a clinical therapy magazine doesn't quite capture the pure joy of EmoTrance and the excitement I have felt for having learned it.

So here are a few Questions and Answers that I hope might lead to a better understanding of EmoTrance, the concepts and beliefs – and also what it is doing for people around the globe...

Is EmoTrance a Therapy?

Yes! But that would be doing EmoTrance a great injustice. Therapies are designed to get you back to square one whilst EmoTrance is designed to make you fly! An EmoTrance practitioner is always looking for the "Energised End State" as an outcome. It's not good enough to be just OK - we want you to feel younger, with more energy as if you are floating on air!

Is EmoTrance a Science?

Yes! But only if you can accept that all living creatures have an energetic/emotional system. Once you make that leap then EmoTrance is completely logical and just makes sense. Like all great discoveries, EmoTrance is simple, natural and you might find you have always been aware of these processes subconsciously.

Is EmoTrance a Healing Technique?

Yes! Doctors of this millennium can work what people just a hundred years ago would consider to be miracles. Yet are we just machines that need to be fixed, or is there something more to us beyond the flesh and bones we can see with our eyes? EmoTrance is about healing everything beyond these dimensions, from your biggest demons to your hopes, dreams and fears. EmoTrance practitioners are the "Spirit Specialists"!

Is EmoTrance a Peak Performance Tool?

Yes! Merely understanding how emotions, body, metaphors and your energetic systems logically interact with each other will give you the edge over your competitors! EmoTrance enabled Peak Performance coaches know how people work on way more of a deeper level and thus are more able to help them achieve there goals.

Is EmoTrance a Philosophy?

Yes! But you don't need to know about this, as the basic levels of EmoTrance will provide most people with the tools of a lifetime! For those who have the time to take a break, look up at the stars and wonder about the wonder of things then EmoTrance will provide you with some key pointers for you to reflect on your own meanings of the world. EmoTrance has been harmoniously designed to be respectful of who you are as a complete individual, including your background and beliefs. And whatever you do believe, EmoTrance allows you to connect yourself more deeply to your soul and the world around you. EmoTrance has been described beautifully as "Taking out a 60 watts bulb, and replacing it with a 100 watts bulb."

I Feel Disassociated with The World/ God/ Lover/ Spouse. Can EmoTrance Help?

Yes! One of the core principals of EmoTrance is that we Human Beings can consciously shield themselves from external sources. EmoTrance teaches you how you can not only let in incoming energies, but also thrive and be energised by them! The EmoTrance process teaches you to heal your systems, not shield them away from the world. Being more connected to the world has a number of benefits from plain enjoyment to a deeper understanding of the Universe and all its complexities.

Can I Learn EmoTrance For Myself?

Yes! The processes EmoTrance works with are completely natural and so just knowing how you respond to events and situations on an energetic/emotional level will give you the edge for processing this information, not shying away or trying to repress it. If there is something you would like help with, then we have hundreds of EmoTrance Practitioners world wide. Remember, an EmoTrance Practitioner works on an energetic level so you do not need to bare your soul to them – unless you want too of course!

Can I Learn EmoTrance For Free?

Yes! All you need to get started can be found on the www.EmoTrance.com website. If you would like a book to read, then 'The EmoTrance Yearbook' is available from the DragonRising.com website as a free download (registration required) or as a low-priced paperback.

Do You Have Any Testimonials? Yes!

The best collection of EmoTrance related reviews and testimonials can be found on www.DragonRising.com under the first EmoTrance book: "Oceans of Energy: The Patterns & Techniques of EmoTrance, Vol 1".

There we go, that feels a lot better for me to summarise EmoTrance than in a mere 200 words! That said, if I really had to cut down EmoTrance to a few words then I'd probably choose:

"Everything Works Better - with EmoTrance!"

Best wishes,

Alex Kent

EmoTrance & The Love Clinic

By Sandra Hillawi, Master Trainer

Recent developments in the field of energy psychology give us a new model for understanding emotions, where they come from, and how to deal with them. Our emotions arise as part of our human response to life experiences but we now understand that emotions are a direct feedback response of the state of the body's subtle energy system.

As we respond to life, what people say and do to us, what happens, what we experience, all this is energy being processed in our energy body, also known as our spiritual body. Just as our body has organs and channels for digesting the food we consume and extracting nourishment from it, and releasing the wastes, so our energy body has centres and systems for handling the energies of life, for deriving nourishment from it and for releasing what we don't need.

When all is flowing in our energy system we get positive emotions: acceptance, understanding, enrichment, clarity, peace, happiness, compassion, joy, delight, rapture and love, the value that life experience has brought us, let's call it energy nutrition.

When we don't handle life so gracefully, maybe because we have so much to handle or we are faced with a huge life event, such as loss or a trauma, these energies build up in our energy system causing a disturbance or blockage. This energy disturbance is now known to be the actual cause of our negative emotions such as anger, guilt pain, hurt, fear, anxiety, sadness, loss, worry accompanied by a physical sensation, pressure or pain in the chest, head, stomach etc. This physical sensation is the location of the blocked energy. And while this energy is blocked, just like we have undigested food sitting in our system, our body, our being cannot derive the benefit until flow and proper processing is restored.

EmoTrance, developed by Silvia Hartmann in 2002, gives us a simple model for understanding how we function as spiritual beings in our environment. EmoTrance gives us a simple natural way of gently releasing the pressure and allowing the energy that had built up to release and flow through the body and out, restoring the even flow, the intensity of negative emotions dissolving in the process.

With EmoTrance when faced with an emotional problem we simply ask 'where do you feel this in your body?' and then we use our intention to soften the energy. As it softens it starts to spread and flow through the body. We have physical sensations such as warmth spreading, coolness flowing, tingling as the energy releases. Once the energy disturbance is released and energy flow restored we feel positive emotions, which arise from states of flow in the energy system.

EmoTrance is a very simple and natural process and can be used on its own or integrated into other therapies. You can also do EmoTrance with anyone anywhere, on a boat, plane, in a restaurant or at a party, (some of my best healing stories have come from these places!) as it's just like having a conversation with someone. People of all ages can benefit even children, who can feel the pressure in the body but don't know how to verbally express their emotions.

Releasing a problem with EmoTrance is mostly content-free which is also a blessing when working with painful memories, where clients don't always want to revisit in detail.

EmoTrance is about real healing that works, based on real feedback from the person in front of you.

But EmoTrance isn't just for healing old injuries simply and elegantly so that life is ok again. EmoTrance gives us SO much more, takes us so much further and beyond in to new experiences of energy joy rapture and delight.

Just as our body has a blueprint or template for health so does our energy body or spirit person. This template is our true potential for how we can live and experience life in its richness and fullness and all the joy and happiness and success that goes with it. The reason we are not living this blueprint is because of past energy blockages from how we handled life in the past, the build up and accumulations of life energies held still in our system and consequent lack of the essential nourishment that our spirit person needs for its health.

By restoring the flow and enabling us to be better nourished by life, EmoTrance moves us closer towards our state of Perfect Even Flow of our template, to our potential as a human being, to our birthright for real love happiness health and success.

Love and Relationships

Relationships are one of the sources of our deepest joy and happiness and also our deepest stress and pain when they go wrong or they end.

Healing and transforming relationships is one of the most rewarding applications for EmoTrance and the following EmoTrance session extract illustrates just how easy it can be to achieve this.

The Love Clinic

Amy had left her relationship 6 weeks earlier, after being with John for 6 months. It was over. John had been under a lot of stress at work and this had put a real strain on their relationship.

After a very difficult period, with a lot of hurt and lack of consideration, Amy decided to leave as she could no longer cope with John's attitude and all physical attraction and desire on Amy's part had completely vanished.

Here's how the session went.

Sandra: So when you think about John's behaviour to you, where do you feel this in your body?

Amy: In my stomach, like a heavy round pressure.

Sandra guides Amy with EmoTrance technique to soften this energy.

Amy: It's spreading out and seems to be flowing downwards to my hips and legs.

Sandra: Where does it want to go next, this energy?

Amy: I feel a warmth travelling down my legs and my feet now feel heavy.

The energy leaves through the toes.

Sandra: So now, when you think about John's behaviour to you, how does it feel?

Amy: It's not so bad, but I still feel a small pressure in the stomach.

Sandra guides Amy as before and the energy travels down the legs and leaves the body again.

Amy: It's ok now, it's like, he can be stressed and I can see that he's not getting at me personally, he's just frustrated with his own issues. It doesn't affect me any more, it just makes me feel I want to support him. I can handle it.

Sandra: So what else bothers you about John?

Sandra & Amy go through all the things that caused Amy to split up from John and apply the same process to locate the energy in the body, soften the energy and watch it flow and release from the body, until there was nothing else about John that Amy could find fault with. Then the investigation turned to their physical relationship.

Sandra: So how much are you attracted to John at the moment? 0 to 10?

Amy: 0 at the moment.

Sandra: So when you think of being intimate with him, where do you feel this in your body?

Amy: In my chest, it's like a barrier.

Amy softens the energy again so that it flows and releases from the body, this time upwards and out through the mouth with the breath.

Sandra: So how much are you attracted to him now?

Amy: 3 out of 10.

Sandra: So there's still a big part of you that isn't attracted to him. Where do you feel this resistance?

Amy: Low down.

Sandra: So lets soften this energy too. Tell me when it is all released ...

Now how strong is your attraction?

Amy: 9 out of 10!*(looking surprised and very pleased)*

Sandra: So there's a tiny bit of you somewhere that doesn't desire him completely, where is that?

Amy: It feels like it's in my head actually, kind of near the side of my forehead.

We soften and release this energy and as you can imagine, we get to 10 out of 10 on desire and a very happy Amy (not to mention a VERY happy John!) as the couple were subsequently reunited.

A Happy Ending

Amy fell in love all over again with John. They reunited, are deeply in love, they moved in together and their relationship and intimacy is also happily restored.

Amy's relationship is flourishing but it could have been over. Amy could have let this relationship go because she was not able to handle what life was presenting her at the time. By restoring flow in her own energy system not only did she strengthen and increase her ability to handle difficult behaviours but at the same time, she could see them for what they were. What was a personal attack and inconsiderate behaviour now was just an expression of frustration in her partner and a need for her understanding and support, which, once clear in herself she then had the resources to give.

Energy Secrets of Relationships

'Energy needs to flow'

and

'Everyone needs energy nutrition'

We can now understand that 'energy needs to flow' means everyone needs to have themselves and their feelings accepted by the other in a relationship, flowing in, through and out. From the acceptance and flow of the energy comes the understanding of what it's about.

When it's hurting us all we know is OUR feeling about it, and we are blocked not only from seeing the other person clearly but in having the resources to be able to respond in a mature or responsible way.

Once the energy is flowing we can SEE what it's all about and can act now in an appropriate way to help the person obviously distressed in front of us. Acceptance of the other person's energy helps it to be released, thus diffusing the energy state and releasing their stress.

'Everyone needs energy nutrition' - When the energy is flowing it delivers to our energy body information, nourishment, understanding, knowledge and a good feeling goes with it. Different energies have different nourishing power just as different foods have different nourishing power. We can be nourished by nature, a spectacular sunset, a kind act or word from a friend. Attention, recognition, appreciation and love are very powerful energies to offer to someone, and are deeply nourishing. This is what we all need and are seeking in our relationships, someone to see us as we are, to appreciate us as we are, to love us as we are. Lets go back and apply this to John and Amy's situation.

Now Amy can handle John's stressed out behaviour, she can see what it's about and feel more compassion for him. Although not recorded in the session, she will now be able to say to him, 'I can see what you're going through, it must be really frustrating for you going through all that day after day at work'. John will feel instant acceptance, instant relief, like 'someone understands me at last and recognises my problem'. The acceptance of his energy by Amy is actually a release channel for his energy and the appreciation in return from Amy is like a soothing balm to his spirit. He feels supported. Stress now released, energy systems back in flow we now have re-connection and mutual understanding once again.

Barriers to Love and Life

Many of us have strong defences and are not open and trusting enough to receive when another pays us a compliment or offers us love. We are suspicious, it's too risky, we were hurt before, and we just won't let someone in again until we are absolutely sure it's safe. This stems from injuries to our energy system sustained in a past experience. Something happened and is still stored in our energy system. We know it. We can feel it. It hurts when we let life in to touch it. Yet despite being closed and guarded we are still looking for, even craving the joy of love in our life.

While we are closed and afraid, protecting ourselves from more injury we cannot experience the real highs and the deep nourishment that is available to us when we let the energy of people in. When that energy streams through us we feel it both physically and emotionally. Every cell tingling, warm and alive with joy and delight.

In Conclusion

EmoTrance gives us a beautiful, simple natural way to repair our energy system of these old injuries, to safely release our shields and barriers so that we can be more open, more courageous, more trusting and reconnect with the world and start to receive the nourishment which we are craving for. EmoTrance gives us a model to understand how life works, how we function in the world around us, to understand ourselves more.

Then we start living more fully, and feeling even more alive, daring to really experience life, not just in our head but in our open heart, deep in our whole being, enriching our soul. And as we open and allow ourselves this nourishment of life, from our environment and from people around us, we become lighter and brighter in ourselves. As bright spirits nourished and shining in our own right we are in a wonderful place to give and to share the best of ourselves with the world around us.

EmoTrance is a gift to help you rediscover the real you, the bright and shiny radiant happier you that you are meant to be and to share and thus a gift for those around you.

Sandra Hillawi, Master Trainer in EmoTrance

Based in Hampshire, UK and Cairo, Egypt.

Information about Sandra's workshops
and training courses internationally visit:
www.passionforhealth.com or tel: +44 (0)2392 433928

EmoTrance Articles

In this section, you can find a variety of EmoTrance introduction articles written by researchers, practitioners and trainers.

Every article highlights one or more important principles of working with EmoTrance.

Even though EmoTrance is surprisingly simple, in this very simplicity there often lies the challenge of overlooking just how many possibilities there are inherent in this way of working with energy.

The following articles will give you an insight not only of the principles of EmoTrance, but of many aspects of working with EmoTrance and real people, in the real world.

EmoTrance & Child Abuse Survivors

by Silvia Hartmann

A psychologist wrote to me and asked if EmoTrance was "suitable to use with treating child abuse survivors". This is what I told them.

I'm also a child abuse survivor and I can attest to the fact that EmoTrance is the gentlest and most helpful form of dealing with the very real "feelings" one is often overcome by, in real time and in the real world.

Indeed, the fact that you don't have to relive anything, actively forgive anything or anyone, and for once you can just go with what your body and your feelings are telling you, and it doesn't matter "if it's real or just imagined" has been a complete godsend to me personally and proven its value and practical helpfulness in many different contexts.

Now, It's Only Energy ...

Now child abuse is a wide and varied thing; it's difficult because the memories as to the exact sequences of events, police memories if you will, are often unclear, skewed, seen through a child's eyes and sometimes just not there, at least not at the top conscious level.

You get dreams and nightmares too, weird flashbacks and all sorts of thoughts over the years and in the end you don't known at all what's what - only that you have all these symptoms and you know something went on that was deeply disturbing.

It is true that one of the reasons I was looking for something that did not rely on conscious awareness and the ability to come up with exact and precise opening statements is because of my personal experiences.

To be able to "cut out all the talk" - and with that, all the justifications, the reasons, the possible flaws in the memories and the arguments, the conflicts and the FEAR of what else might be there - was a positive GODSEND to me. After all these years, I was tired of telling and talking. I was tired of even thinking about how and if and what. I was tired of remembering and trying to remember. It got me nowhere and often, I used to think, "My God that was nearly half a century ago - will it EVER be over?!"

EmoTrance works with energy and this explains why time wasn't healing this - the energy system is timeless in essence, all things are here and now, and until and unless something is DONE to change the conditions of the energy system, things will remain just as they were forever.

At the same time, there is the other side of the coin. All "that" isn't here any longer. It is all gone, long gone and the ONLY place in which these injuries still exist are indeed, in the energy system. That is a wonderfully soothing thought, and when waves of painful emotions hit you, to be able to think, "This is ONLY AN ENERGY now, and there is something I can do about that!" has been a revelation to me and so many others.

Coming Home To The Body

To be able to validate my "weird" emotional responses to "perfectly normal" situations was also immensely helpful. In EmoTrance we take the point of view that we were ONLY dealing with energy now and disturbances in the energy system; this allowed me to accept the emotions, feelings and sensations for what they really were: cries for help, the sign posts to direct me straight towards what needed healing and restoring.

For the first time, rather than having to switch off my body sensations, I could finally listen to them, acknowledge them and USE THEM for arrow straight guided self healing.

Starting to actively pay attention to my physical feelings which are what emotions really are got me "back into the body" for the first time in 45 years. The body was no longer the enemy; instead, it had become a system crying out for help, and finally, these cries for help could be heard, and then answered with action. This action starts with a healing intention and all else flows from there. Further, the act of listening and paying attention to the actual body sensations that we call feelings and emotions is the perfect guideline to your own custom made healing therapy. As each sensation emerges and is dealt with, the healing process unfolds under its own steam, in its own ecology, in the right order and sequence and WITHOUT FEAR or any kind of major abreaction, major operations, re-traumatizing flashbacks and entirely in harmony with every individual person and their particular needs.

Innocent Energy

EmoTrance is amazing in its presuppositions and in how it works.

There's nothing quite like it, and the totally NON-JUDGEMENTAL nature of all its workings, which for some people seems strange and even sometimes too logical and systemic, is exactly what the doctor ordered for child abuse survivors, and especially child SEX abuse survivors.

Any healing modality that is going to work with child sex abuse survivors has to be ABSOLUTELY systemic and non-judgemental or else the aspects who hold all that shame and guilt and grief and anger and hatred simply CANNOT benefit from any healing - they are structurally excluded "because they don't deserve to be healed".

And of course, I don't even want to begin to start talking about the aspects who may have identified with the abuser/s, developed Stockholm syndrome, connected to them or patterned themselves on them in some way - those never get a look in the standard approaches of psychotherapy and many other doctrines of psychology and spiritual healing.

In EmoTrance, we don't have "good" or "bad" energies. All is ONLY ENERGY. That's just like you can't stand in the rain, watch the raindrops go by and point a finger and say, "Look there goes another bad one!"

This is the concept of "innocent energy" - rain will fall on an abuser and their victims, on the grass and the mountains just the same, it makes no judgement either way. For abuse survivors, this concept can be life saving, for every abuse survivor is both the abuser and the victim in one person.

In EmoTrance, we don't have to struggle for forgiveness or self forgiveness. The whole concept dissolves the moment the pain is gone - once that happens, forgiveness comes into being. It is important to understand that it is STRUCTURALLY IMPOSSIBLE to forgive yourself or any other whilst you are still in acute pain. When the pain has ceased, forgiveness arises naturally - and not one moment earlier.

We can call our emotions what we like - shame, guilt, anger, fear, hatred, disgust, sadness, depression; but in the end, these are all just pain deriving from injuries in the energy system.

Pain we feel in our bodies, pain which shows us where we need to direct our healing intention and our healing energy.

Shields & Abuse Survivors

Of course, the more you have been hurt, the more shielded you become – it's an automatic process that happens without any volition, just like a callous will grow over an injury to protect that area in the physical body.

I have often been told that I need to be more trusting, or that I should be more connected, or less shielded – but I never knew

HOW to do that, I had no idea. I had also no idea how I was supposed to "let more love into my life" or even "accept love when it is offered".

For an abuse survivor, that is adding insult to injury. How do you tell a callous not to grow? Shields are not the problem, they are the RESULT of painful injuries sustained; to be able to function at all and to survive in spite of such life-threatening injuries, shields are of the essence. They are a protective device, something that should be there only for a short time and then, when the injury has healed, it is supposed to dissolve all by itself.

Only, the REAL injuries haven't been healed; and the numbness around the very places where the worst injuries are "hiding" makes it very difficult to do anything about that or make any forward movements towards healing – until EmoTrance, that is.

It is very easy to start identifying shields once you've seen a few; and also, you can just simply ask a person – where are your shields to love, joy and happiness? Show me with your hands. Sometimes when you do that, the person shakes their head and says, "I don't know ..." but their hands have already lifted and shown you exactly where the shield is to be found. I say, "Just stop there for a moment ... look at your own hands!" Then they become aware of it and sometimes they're shocked at first, that their hands know and they want to help, but it is also a wonderful example of how our body is not and never was our enemy, but in the contrary, or greatest champion and ally who will never, ever stop fighting for us, until we draw our last breath on this earth.

Behind the shields, there lie the big injuries. EmoTrance is gentle and it proceeds no faster than a person is ready to go; we make microscopic holes in the shield at first so we can find out where the injury is, so that it may be healed at last. Then, and when it doesn't hurt anymore, it is easy to take down the shield, because now, we don't need it anymore.

Once this process begins, there is hope again. The first event is "a taste of healing", and with every injury healed, with every shield removed, we become more connected to the world, and more nourished by it – in absolute safety and eventually, in real joy.

Recovering The Love Of Life

It is true that when I first began to experiment with EmoTrance, I had no idea that it would do so much more than just really heal the worst forms of emotional pain. To even find some minor relief for this everlasting chronic suffering that child abuse survivors have learned to live with somehow would have been akin to a miracle to me.

But EmoTrance goes much, much further than that.

There is another side, something beyond "just not feeling the pain anymore".

Once we begin to listen to the body again and end the withdrawal from the physical, to our amazement we find that the body can send us other kinds of feedback about the energy system - the good feelings. When the energy system is working once more as it should, as it was designed to work by the Creative Order, and we have learned to listen again, we become the recipients of wonderful gifts. Feelings of joy, of energies rushing through your body, making you tingle, making you feel alive and powerful, opening your eyes to the beauty of the world and your place within it - it is extraordinary to come home to that at last.

That is the greatest gift of EmoTrance for me - to end my long exile and allow me to come home to Creation itself.

In Conclusion

All the re-unification processes of EmoTrance, all the weight on the systemic nature and structure of injuries in the energy system and how they relate firstly to emotion, and from there manifest in thought and behaviour that are at the core of EmoTrance were first of all road tested right there - in the abuse survivor scenarios, in the high end trenches of psychological and energetic disturbance that have lasted a lifetime.

Further still, the "client - practitioner dance" at the heart of the co-joint healing endeavour between two EQUALS, where the "healer" is literally FORBIDDEN to tell anyone what is wrong with them or how they "should" be feeling, and where the healers are ONLY allowed to focus on "putting to right what once went wrong", only FOLLOW ALONG with the person's own special unfoldments and even then, ONLY when and if the person in question is ready and willing, all that is patterned directly on the needs of child abuse survivors.

Of course, these "fail safes" build right into the very structure of EmoTrance are of benefit to ANYONE AT ALL, and it doesn't matter why they are in pain or where they got their disturbances from.

EmoTrance is not an instant miracle cure for child abuse survivors; but I can personally attest to the fact that every aspect of its theory, workings, structure and how EmoTrance is conducted is designed to help child abuse survivors finally find relief for their emotions and injuries, and to put them on the road to have all the pleasures of life, all the wonderful experiences of the body, back in their reach when it seemed so impossible before.

© Silvia Hartmann 2003/2007

Emotional Eating, Emotional Overeating - Why Do Our Feelings Make Us Eat?

by Louise Bliss

Emotional Eating, Emotional Overeating - Why Do Our Feelings Make Us Eat? Understanding how your EMOTIONS affect your WEIGHT is one thing and to ask if your past hold the KEY to your DIETING HABITS is another. But here is a far more direct route to get control of emotional overeating and emotional eating - here is something NEW that really works to make those hungry emotions literally disappear.

There are many theories on the causes of why we emotional eat. You will read and listen to many views including both psychological and physiological reasons - but at the end of the day it is FEELINGS that drive us to the fridge or the cupboard, feelings of need, of hunger, feeling we don't want to feel and we know we can make them go away when we eat something, feelings that are so strong that we can't ignore them or fight them off with willpower - and that is what leads to emotional overeating.

We can set out with all good intentions when trying to lose weight, going to a diet club, throwing out everything in the cupboards, going to the supermarket armed with a healthy shopping list, feeling extremely smug when looking at other shoppers trolley's full of pizza, burgers, chips and various processed meals and joining that gym thinking this is it, this is the time when I crack whatever it is that is stopping me being at my goal weight. It's all about healthy eating, exercise and nothing more!

Then BANG something comes along to rock your world and that highly motivated beginning has disappeared.

The REASON - there's is something else, another part of the equation, your feelings, your EMOTIONS and how they affect you in your everyday life including your quest to LOSE WEIGHT and keep it off.

So do you want to master your EMOTIONS and BREAK this ongoing cycle once and for all?

As humans we have our physical body with all its systems, however we also have an ENERGY body and our physical body give us the feedback as to where we are storing our emotions that may affect us with all sorts of LIFE ISSUES but for now we will focus on breaking FREE from our ongoing WEIGHT LOSS battle.

Going on a DIET to many people often means living a restrictive lifestyle, making radical dietary changes, cutting out certain food groups and missing out on having fun, parties etc. This often can leave you feeling FRUSTRATED, STRESSED, ANXIOUS, and even DEPRESSED. So then all your good intentions go to waste because you tell yourself things like "what's the point", "nothing ever changes", "I knew it wouldn't work", "I am useless" and the list goes on. You then unfortunately go back to your old habits. Does all this sound familiar?

SO what if you could MASTER your emotions and break the habits that affect you and your WEIGHT?

You CAN with EMOTRANCE. EMOTRANCE it is a fantastic simple, YET VERY PROFOUND technique that anyone can use in any moment when emotions are running high and threatening to overwhelm to literally transform emotions from feeling bad to feeling good instead. EmoTrance is extremely powerful and amazingly effective at stopping emotional overeating.

One aspect of understanding how your emotions affect you and your weight is to look at your past, go back as far as you can remember, acknowledge events, issues, and incidents that had an impact on your life and look at how they affected you emotionally. The FANTASTIC thing with EMOTRANCE is that no matter how old, how painful the problem is EMOTRANCE can work swiftly and give you very instant emotional transformational results. So once you have indentified the main EMOTIONS from the past, you can use the techniques to clear each and every past hurt, giving you EMOTIONAL FREEDOM to assist you with LOSING WEIGHT and all its many challenges.

So if you want to learn how to eat what you love and not gain WEIGHT, Stop CRAVINGS, obsessions and compulsions in just a few minutes, get and stay motivated to LOSE WEIGHT then use EMOTRANCE to help stop the struggle and gain CONTROL.

EMOTRANCE is very accessible you can start by taking a look at www.emotrance.com or by reading "Oceans of Energy" by Silvia Hartmann the founder of EMOTRANCE. You can also visit an EmoTrance practitioner who is an energy specialist and their role is to work with you and help you take charge of your emotions, tackle the root causes of weight gain and break the ongoing cycle of DIETING so that emotional overeating becomes a thing of the past.

Louise Bliss
Emotional Freedom Training
www.emotionalfreedom-training.co.uk
+44 (0)208 845 1293 / +44(0)7811 447070

Dyslexia Help With EmoTrance

by Sandra Hillawi

Could this be a new breakthrough treatment for dyslexia? Whilst a few individual successful cases is very encouraging, we can't make any general claims. However, these results indicate research in this area would certainly be very worthwhile. Here are 3 cases of helping people successfully with the symptoms of dyslexia including writing down numbers, reading, and comprehension.

Working with EmoTrance over the years I have had the opportunity to work with a number of people who said they were dyslexic. When explored with an EmoTrance approach, namely locating blocked emotional energy and releasing it, quite amazing improvements and results have been obtained, literally in minutes.

Dyslexia Case 1: Dyslexic Since Childhood

The latest case which prompts my article was during my last Thursday weekly workshop. It was a real hallelujah moment...

The story : Jackie was dyslexic from childhood and until now had difficulties reading and writing things down under instruction.

She described it as a wall coming down in front of her when she was asked to do such a task, that had started when she was at school. It was reinforced by the way her parents treated her and how she came to feel 'thick', 'not good enough' and 'trapped and limited' by the condition.We first did some energy releasing about her anger and resentment towards her parents for how they dealt with it. Then we came to how she felt about her self having dyslexia. There was anger and hurt, in the chest, we softened and flowed. The energy released down her arm and out. I asked again, and we released until she could accept herself with the dyslexia. It was now ok to have it.

I then asked how much did she love herself with the dyslexia 0-10? She smiled and said 8. So we located the energy of the last part that didn't love herself and released this until she loved herself completely.

Next I asked...the concept of your dyslexia, where does it live? She put her hands on her chest. We softened and flowed. The energy released up and out of her head. I asked again. Its gone she said. How does that feel to you? I asked. Its strange, she said. Where is this strange feeling? In my chest, she said. Ok, let's soften and flow this. The energy released. She smiled, and said ...it feels....normal. Its gone, I feel like I'm normal, like everyone else. I noticed her getting emotional, the energy building in her chest , we softened, the energy flowed up and out. She was quite joyful at this stage.

I asked her about what activities her dyslexia made difficult for her. She said...when someone asks me to write something down. It happened last week. So I got some paper out and told her I was going to ask her to write something. She was eager and ready, but felt a pressure in the chest. We stopped to soften and release this energy which went down the arm and out. I repeated my statement of intention, she was eagerly ready now to try. I dictated, she started to write. I asked what's going on now? She said I have a pressure in my shoulder. We stopped to soften and flow and release this energy. She continued to write. We repeated this a few times until there was no disturbance whatsoever in her body while writing things down. She was amazed. This was a first for as long as she could remember.

So I asked what other activities are difficult because of the dyslexia? Reading, she replied.So I gave her something to read and asked her to observe what was happening in her body. She said I have a pressure in my head, around my eyes. We softened, flowed, the energy released up and out. She continued and she was able to read in a relaxed way, understanding all that she read.Our workshop time ended with a delighted Jackie and a very impressed audience so we will see how she puts this to the test during the next week.

Other cases I have worked with were similar.

Dyslexia Case 2: Difficulties Reading & Absorbing Information

Susan had difficulties absorbing information and said she felt pain at the back of her head and sometimes pressure in her lower back when she tried to read. She said she started having difficulties around age 11. I said did anything else happen round that time? She said she had a fall, rolled down a hill, banged her head and that was a bit frightening at the time. I asked where she felt pain in her body when she recalled this fall?

She said the back of her head, same place as the pressure she felt when trying to read.So we released the energy of the trauma from the fall at age 11, then proceeded to locate and release the energies she felt in her head and her back when trying to read. At the end she was amazed at how she was so relaxed reading and she could take the information in and understand it. A new lease of life had just begun, being able to read and learn.

Dyslexia Case 3: Writing Down Numbers

During another EmoTrance Training I had a lady, Mary, with dyslexia. During the break I asked if we could explore the energetics of her problem with EmoTrance. We didn't have much time, maybe 10-15 minutes. The first thing we explored was what happens in her body when she tried to read something, like the poster on the wall with the small print. She had a pressure at the top of her head. We softened and flowed, released the pressure. Again, we repeated this process until she could read the whole paragraph on the wall poster relaxed and easily. She was amazed.

Her other problem was writing down numbers. I asked her to write my phone number down and tell me what happens. She started to write the first number then got stuck on the second. She said it felt black in front of her eyes and a pressure inside her head. We softened and flowed the energy from the inside of the head. For the black energy in front of her eyes, we softened and brought this energy in through and out of her body. Again, I dictated the number and we repeated until she wrote the whole number down with ease. We tested with a few telephone numbers.

Mary was getting very emotional about the results we were having and the implications of change after so many years struggling. That was all in the chest. We softened flowed and released til she felt happy and relaxed.

In this case the problem did return. As I stated, we did this as an quick exploration in a 15 minute break, so I didn't have the chance to be thorough as I did with Jackie in Case 1 or Susan in Case 2.

What is interesting about these cases is how locating the blocked energy related to the task and releasing it, made the task so much easier. It was very encouraging to see the dramatic improvements in the dyslexic cases as a result of using the EmoTrance approach to releasing emotional energy about the tasks and the speed of achievement of results.

Could this be a new breakthrough treatment for dyslexia? Whilst a few individual successful cases is very encouraging, we can't make any general claims. However, these results indicate research in this area would certainly be very worthwhile.

In fact, any task we perform, can be improved in the same way, by paying attention to what's happening in the body while we perform the task, identifying these energy blockages in and around the body, and releasing them with our intention for the energy to soften and flow.

Sandra Hillawi
Master Trainer of EmoTrance
www.sandrahillawi.com

Negative Energies – Just A Misconception?

by Detlev Tesch, EmoTrance Trainer

Since I first learned about the energy worlds I have been confronted with the concept of "positive and negative energies". So many healers, intuitives, clairvoyants, and people in general talk and write about it. You will find lots of books and websites that tell you how important it is to focus on positive energies and avoid negative ones, shield them off, and avoid people, things and places that emanate negative energies.

Life With Negative Energies

And don't we all experience those negative energies on a more or less daily basis? Those negative people and their negative talk. Lots of negative news in the newspapers, on the radio, and on the TV. Dreadful co-workers, awful customers or clients, unfriendly staff in shops, offices, agencies etc.

So, the idea of negative energies has been with me for years and I found powerful proof that they exist:

A few years ago I had fallen in love with a woman and she with me. After we had known each other for only a few weeks we had the opportunity to spend a two week holiday in Tuscany. Oh, what an exquisite joy for two so freshly and deeply in love.

We had a nice romantic little apartment in a lovely place. The weather was just ideal. We had great food in nice restaurants. We were really having a most wonderful time and lots of fun.

It was hard to imagine anything more "positive" than that.

One day, filled with all that happiness and excitement, we were on an excursion to some beautiful town in Tuscany. We had parked my car outside the city walls and on this magnificent day in late August we were, hand in hand, happily, merrily walking narrow busy streets towards the city centre.

All of a sudden I felt an abrupt mood-swing. There was a mix of emotions like anger, sadness, rage, and more that I do not remember. There was no apparent reason for this at all.

Boy, had I been glad then that I had taken all those seminars in a specific energy healing modality. Thus I knew that the emotions we feel are not always our own, but can be emotional energies that we catch like a cold. Ok, that by itself was informative, but did not allow me to change things. But I knew, what else to do and how to do it: Create and program a powerful energy shield to ward of negative energies, then cleanse myself of the energies I had caught and that were making me feel bad.

So I ushered my girlfriend into an alley and briefly explained the situation. Then I did what I had to do to establish that shield and the got rid of those strange energies.

This whole episode may have taken somewhere between 5 and 10 minutes, and then I was back to my happy, loving self and could now, again, enjoy the day, the gorgeous weather, the beautiful town and my charming girlfriend.

If I had needed any more proof that negative energies exist, this had been it.

And in the years to come there were more situations, if not as impressive, that supported the concept of negative energies.

Maybe some of you can relate to this: Going shopping or running errands in a busy city or shopping centre can be a very draining experience. I used to notice that I felt exhausted after a few hours in town, especially in bad or hot weather, around Christmas etc. when people tend to be particularly stressed out. All too often I would get home with a headache, bad mood, on some occasions even feeling depressed.

At times I would avoid this by putting up a strong energy shield. Yet often I simply forgot. In retrospect I can say, that at times it somehow did NOT FEEL RIGHT to put one up – for whatever the reason. Thus there were many, many opportunities for a bit of suffering.

And with all the books and articles and seminars talking about negative energies, what they do to us, and how we can protect ourselves from them – and that we ought to do that for the sake of our positive spiritual development – this quite simply was part of my reality.

Now Enter EmoTrance ...

It seems that I have been directed towards EmoTrance by higher forces, much like I had been directed towards learning energy healing years before. And EmoTrance felt so right, right from the beginning. But there was this strange idea saying "There is no GOOD or BAD [just other words for "positive" and "negative"] energy, there is ONLY ENERGY".

On a deeper level this immediately rang true. On the conscious level, however, I encountered a contradiction. This statement contradicted what I had learned in years of energy work AND it contradicted my very own experiences: There ARE bad, negative energies and we do have to shield them off. This had been proven in Tuscany, hadn't it?

Well, let's think again and take a closer look.

What happens in our bodies, in our energy systems when we experience bad, negative, unpleasant feelings about some energy? There is a build-up of energy that cannot flow properly. This creates energetic "pressure". This pressure then turns into a kinaesthetic sensation that hurts us or feels uncomfortable. EmoTrance theory says that our systems were designed to handle ANY naturally occurring energy (from objects, plants, animals, humans, environments, etc.) so that we can take whatever is beneficial from them and let the rest flow out.

Aha! So what this means is: If an energy cannot be channelled or processed correctly, then we have a negative i.e. an unpleasant experience.

Alright, so the "negative" quality is not inherent in the energy itself but derives from problems in our very own energy systems.

Wow, what an eye opener. What a fresh perspective. That makes real sense!

And how empowering that is! If there are "bad" energies "out there" and there is nothing we can do but avoid them (or if we're lucky we find a technique somewhere to "transform" them), our choices are very limited.

If on the other hand we OWN the problem, we can do something about it. We can heal ourselves. We can make ourselves stronger. We can "grow" and become powerful enough so that we no longer need to be scared and no longer need to avoid that energy.

If we heal ourselves using EmoTrance we win immensely.

We can heal a problem that might even be very old or severe and it usually is fast and easy.

We stop the suffering and the discomfort.

We can energetically "feed" on the energy that used to be a threat to us.

This means that we can use FOR OUR WELL-BEING what used to give us a hard time!

We can even get an energized end state and feel absolutely wonderful. Now, is that cool, or is that cool?

Even if we might not go that far every time, the thing is that we now have more options than we used to!

Having options to choose from is FREEDOM.

Life with EmoTrance

So, what difference does this make in daily life?

Let's take the situation of going shopping in a buzzing town.

It happened last march in Bonn, where I live. A beautiful spring day. I was downtown for several hours. There was some special festivity and the city centre was packed with people. People shopping, people hurrying, calling, shouting... There were loads of activities, musicians, and performers. Cafés and terraces were crowded. There were more happy, smiling faces than usual, but the grim ones still held the vast majority.

Then I noticed that my mood was on a downswing. Just like that. But this time I had help. No, it wasn't Superman, nor Wonder Woman, not Spiderman, or Mr. Incredible and no energy shield either. It was EmoTrance that came to my rescue.

Soften and flow – while I am still making my way through the crowds. Soften and flow and no one knows what I am doing to myself. Soften and flow and there is an almost instantaneous shift. A moment later I feel fine again. A smile shows up on my face. Ah, there's a few people responding, smiling back... Wonderful... How much better people look when they are smiling!

Please note: There was no need for me, to transform those masses of supposedly negative emotions and energies that were amassed there by hundreds, even thousands of people (an overwhelming task, if you ask me). I did not need to run away from that situation either. Nor was there any necessity to shield myself and forego all that energy nutrition. I could do what I had come for, I could enjoy the day, I could feel good, no matter what was going on for all the other people, what they were feeling, what energies they were emanating.

I was free to stay or to leave.

I was free from suffering.

The energies could not drive me away.

This is more powerful and liberating than any other concept I have come across.

Or take any unpleasant situation at work – like being criticised by a supervisor or co-worker.

Normally our body has a stress reaction to that. This leads to all sorts of substances being poured into our blood stream. Among those is adrenalin. One of the effects adrenalin has is that it blocks synaptic communication in our brain to varying degrees. As a consequence we cannot think clearly, we cannot access memories effectively etc. (Ever been in an exam and forgotten what you had learned? Then you know what I'm talking about!)

This means: We become stress stupid – more or less, depending on how severe the stress reaction is. Due to stress we tend to do stupid things, say stupid things and make stupid decisions.

For this reason we rarely find good solutions in such a situation; indeed, in the contrary, we often make things even worse.

Now, with EmoTrance we can soften and flow our emotional reaction on the spot, right there and then, right here and now. We can have more or all of our intelligence at our command.

We can make better choices and find better solutions.

And on top of all that: we can feel much better.

And we haven't even touched on the subject of treating and resolving patterns of emotional reactions outside of acute situations and how beneficial, how life changing, that can be.

So: YES, the concept of "negative energies" is nothing but a misconception, albeit a very widespread one. There is ONLY ENERGY. If it hurts, then there's an injury or a blockage. And that can be healed.

And now you who know EmoTrance, you might just as well forget all about "negative energies"

Just be ready to soften and flow. Be ready to be happy. Be ready to enjoy life.

You don't know how to do EmoTrance yet?

Do not worry.

It's easy to learn and easy to do.

And there are more and more workshops you can go to.

Welcome to the enchanted world of EmoTrance!

Diplom.-Ökonom Detlev Tesch, November 2007

Detlev Tesch
EmoTrance Trainer
Tesch Coaching & Training
Kuedinghovener Str. 142
53227 Bonn, Germany
www.webtesch.de
www.EmoTrance.eu

EmoTrance and Reiki

By Nicola Quinn, Reiki Master

EmoTrance is not just an amazing technique on its own, it works beautifully with ALL other energy therapies and modalities.

I would even go further than that and say there is NOTHING that EmoTrance can not enhance or increase the positive benefits of and this includes all spiritual practices, be it meditation, prayer, or the daily Course in Miracles exercises.

All paths give specific instructions as to what to do to attain enlightenment - love yourself, forgive yourself, be positive, be more connected, feel compassion for others, become more connected to the all-there-is etc - but they don't actually tell you HOW to do this.

As an example I have found EmoTrance extremely useful, in fact ESSENTIAL, in preparing students for their Reiki attunements and as an integral part of Reiki treatments.

Years ago when I received my Reiki attunements I had so many emotional and physical issues the attunements themselves sent me into a spiral of increased physical and emotional discomfort from which I found having Reiki to call upon a double edged sword and initially I was very reticent about using my new skill for fear of feeling any worse!

I was determined when I offered Reiki attunements that NO-ONE should suffer as I had done.

So as part of the training I give I use EmoTrance to remove blockages in the energy system and to establish an evenflow of energy which allows Reiki to flow beautifully through the entire system without causing pain or discomfort, the classic 'Reiki sickness' which follows so many attunements.

One reason, I am certain, that this sickness occurs after attunements is because we each have our own individual fault lines, weak ereas that respond to stress in the same way, over and over, day in day out, becoming ever more fragile and susceptible over time. These ereas, these stress fractures, need healing before any type of energy can be tolerated without a huge flare up of the same old symptoms and this EmoTrance pinpoints for elegant and swift resolution.

But EmoTrance goes even further than clearing old pains and injuries, it prepares the student to accept the awe-inspiring fact that they are about to become a powerful and effective healer.

This for some is mind-blowing.

How would YOU deal with that?

If I say to you that within the week you will have powerful healing energy flowing from your hands to heal yourself, your family, your friends, where do you feel that in your body? What sort of emotions do you feel right now with that thought? To many that's a daunting prospect.

To be able to EmoTrance that through and reach the energized end state where that thought literally makes you tingle all over is the ideal receptive state to be in to receive the attunements and move forward as a healer in a confident, congruent way.

Then there are the Reiki treatments themselves, another chance to see EmoTrance in superb action.

As with all healing modalities, emotions can run high as muscles, holding years of trauma, begin to relax and release their memories. Thoughts and feelings float up as they are triggered by the work in progress and sometimes this can be overwhelming for the client, and practitioner alike, without knowledge of EmoTrance and how to encourage a softening and flowing of the heavy burdens just released.

EmoTrance gives Reiki healers the confidence to deal with any emotional situation, as it arises, for the client and themselves, and is a priceless skill to have in a therapeutic setting.

And it works the other way round too! Reiki is a perfect adjunct to EmoTrance, it is superb for healing fault lines and stress fractures and warm Reiki hands certainly lend themselves nicely to dissolving blocks of energy and helping to initiate an even flow of energy.

As one of my Reiki students, Daniel Escamilla, so beautifully put it when he wrote to me after taking my Reiki course having prepared for his attunements using EmoTrance.

"I am amazed how well I feel, and how my interactions with people at work and all over seems to improve. I didn't realize how stuck I was in receiving a compliment from people, doing the exercises has removed many of those blockages, that may have been there for a very long time. How wonderful to receive even a "Hello" from some one and let it flow, and get to that wonderful state, as energy zips by.

Nicola, I had believed that Reiki or energy goes where it is needed, now as I experience the energy flowing through blockages, I can say for sure, "I know it" from experience, not just theory. I sense your spirit and kindness guiding me, as I clear. Thank you very much. I truly love your practical approach and the experiential knowledge of actually feeling in my body the energy, instead of just in my head, thinking or theory, by combining Reiki with EmoTrance."

And, as I mentioned in the introduction, how anyone can achieve spiritual discipline, let alone enlightenment without EmoTrance is a mystery to me.

Just try forgiving someone who has caused you deep pain without the power of EmoTrance behind you. It can be strenuous and time consuming, time we do not have now. With EmoTrance we have found that once a channel is clear that that same movement, that same emotion, becomes easier and quicker to process, energy in and straight out, eventually becoming automatic.

We need to be able to clear out all our cobwebs, let our energy systems run clear, clean and bright so we can get on with living our lives and really making a positive contribution to the world.

And EmoTrance and Reiki work beautifully, hand in hand, to accomplish this sacred task.

Nicola Quinn
EmoTrance Co-Developer & Reiki Master
http://nicolaquinn.com

EmoTrance & Spirituality - A Christian Perspective

by Margarita Foley, EmoTrance Trainer

Over 20 years ago during a stay in Japan I met a young American man who was studying Buddhism and learning Japanese as I was at that time. Each day in our lunch break we had many discussions on the meaning of life and so forth. One day he said to me, "What is important is to be in the flow of your being."

At that time I did not understand the meaning of this but I pondered it very often. I was puzzled and wondered how that could be true for me. Then one day I passed by a moat in the grounds of the Old Imperial Castle in Kyoto. As I watched the water flowing I began to understand what "going with the flow of your being" means. It means that we keep flowing on day by day at ease and in peace in our deepest core. This life is a journey we take and we learn as we flow.

And I again heard the word in 2002 when I first heard of Emotional Freedom Technique. I learned that energy is meant to flow and when it is blocked it needs to be released. Through a system of tapping on the acupuncture points on the body while tuning into the 'problem' it is possible to release blocked energy. When I learned this it seemed miraculous and my interest in this kind of energy work was engaged. Of course I already had experience of and training in reflexology, Indian Head Massage and Reiki healing. In fact energy has fascinated me for years.

It began when I learned to pray. At first I learned to say prayers and then I joined with my family in the recitation of the Rosary, a prayer that was familiar to many Irish Catholic families when I was a child. It consists of 5 decades of prayer asking Mary Mother of Jesus to pray with us as we meditated on different episodes of the life journey of Jesus. Because I wanted to avoid the boredom that the rhythm of this prayer induced I began to visualize each of the scenes and entered into the story myself. I would hold conversations with the different characters. In this way I began to enjoy saying the Rosary with my family. Later this was a great resource when faced with life decisions.

I realized that real prayer is about relationship with the source of my being. At first this was a simple relationship with the person of Jesus as I perceived him. Later I began to understand that Jesus was the perfect reflection of God who is the Source of being or the Father. What is known as the Holy Spirit is the Breath of Love between the Father and the Son.

I also learned that each one of these plays a different role in the relationship and that they are Persons - Divine Persons. That is why we say One God and Three Persons. But for me the fascinating point is that there is a completely free flow of Love between the Three Persons. Now it is possible to have all kinds of interesting discussions about whether they are persons like we are.

All we can say is that they are Personal Beings who allow their love to flow evenly and completely from one to the other and that love flows through to us through the One who is the Expression of Love that is the person known as Jesus. Since he became human, our humanity is joined to the flow of the Three Persons.

As a Catholic I learned that I have become a member of Christ or a follower of Christ when I was baptised. This means that I have entered into the flow of the relationship. But because I am incarnate in a human body I have inherited all kinds of human weaknesses and hang-ups. These can disrupt the flow of love in my life in all areas, in my perception, in my relationships, in my behaviour, in my activities and even in my relationship with my

Source. This has often caused me distress and also made me search for answers.

In 2002 I was also invited to the very first presentation of EmoTrance at the Commonwealth Centre in London. For various reasons I was unable to be present. But I felt a movement of deep joy and excitement when I heard about it. I remember a conversation with Nicola Quinn and she became aware of my enthusiasm. Moreover the seeming simplicity of the technique attracted me as I am a creature who loves simple ways. (Of course what appears simple at first can have an amazing complexity in its possibility as I am now discovering.)

In 2003 I received the invitation to the EmoTrance training with Nicola Quinn and Silvia Hartmann. My whole being answered "Yes" as I glimpsed the wonder hidden in EmoTrance.

I was just emerging from the pain of the loss of two beloved brothers who died at a relatively young age. I became aware of the 'blockage' the grief was creating in me and was overjoyed to release the energy of this deeply held grief. I noticed too how my perception and insight changed as my energy was flowing more freely.

EmoTrance enhanced what I had experienced in my life previously. I believe there is a Spirit or Energy connection between everything in the Universe. This is an intuition I have had from very early in my life. All of the great writers have attempted to convey this, for example, "Nothing is either good or bad, but thinking makes it so."

An Irish poet, called Joseph Mary Plunkett wrote a poem called the "Presence of God".

He says,

> *"I see his Blood upon the rose*
> *And in the stars the glory of His eyes,*
> *His body gleams amid eternal snows,*
> *His tears fall from the skies ..."*

And even though I have felt the emotional impact that different wars and unrest is having on us as humans I can never stop believing in the possibility for each of us to return to the flow of our original being.

At first when practising EmoTrance I had some difficulty getting in touch with the flow of energy, which can be quite subtle. There were times when I asked myself if it was for real! But I kept practising and gradually I began to realize the truly powerful effect of releasing blocked energy.

And this is not all. We also need to find energy in so many areas of our lives. It may be healing from the hurts of life, the energy of forgiveness, or the energy of love, or the ability to learn by immersion in the energy of what we want to learn. As those of us who are practioners and trainers are discovering there seems to be no end to the ways in which EmoTrance can be used.

Let me tell you about how it has helped me to grow spiritually.

In the area of forgiveness I had tried so many ways, breathing in the forgiveness of Jesus and drawing in light and love through breath. So when I learned EmoTrance I decided to test it on the most holistic prayer I have as a Christian – The Our Father.

I took each single phrase of the Our Father and allowed the energy of this to flow through me.

With the words "Our Father who art in Heaven" I allow the energy of the flow of the Three Persons to flow through my being. This brings the prayer right into my energy and into my body. I began to experience something of peace and harmony and where I noticed blocks in myself I allowed them to soften and flow. And yes, we can feel blocks to the energy of love, even pure love!

I continue to take each phrase in turn, "May the holiness/wholeness of your name flow through me." I allow "Your Kingdom of peace, justice and healing" to flow through me and into the world in which I live. And of course I have to let the energy of the blockages that I see in me and in the world around me soften and flow frequently.

The energy of the words, "Your will be done on earth as it is in heaven" mean that we allow and work for the creation of a more peaceful, loving, just and harmonious world. For this I need to continually allow this energy to flow through me to myself, to other people and situations where this energy is required. Again the words "Give us this day our daily bread". There are so many things we need at each moment and it is not necessarily food. We need all kinds of things even things we would not consider very nourishing and as we allow the energy to flow through we are allowing all the good things we need to flow to us, and through us to the wider universe.

Again the words, "Forgive us our sins as we forgive those who sin/hurt/injure us" taught me to allow the energy of forgiveness to heal me and to flow through me to people who hurt or injured me. There are constant opportunities here to practice EmoTrance on the emotions which prevent us from forgiving and which so often lead to distress and ill-health.

"Lead us not into temptation" feels old fashioned until I realize how easy it is to be tempted to power which draws me away from unconditional love. Or the attraction of lust may tempt me away from the joy and the struggle of real love. So EmoTrance comes to my rescue and increases my joy in so many ways. Yes I can say with my hand on my heart that EmoTrance is such a great gift to me and has enabled me to grow much stronger as a human being. It has enabled me to live my spirituality in an incarnate way.

Each person has a journey to make and each of our experiences is different. EmoTrance enables each of us to open the pathways to a deeper understanding of ourselves and each other. It is a pathway to greater power, love and creativity in our lives, whether we are politicians, therapists, prisoners, builders or little children. You too will discover how EmoTrance will bring great joy and delight along the way.

EmoTrance can enable us to appreciate the power that is ours and all that we can achieve when our energy is flowing freely the way it needs to flow.

For this I can only say a big "Thank You" to the Source and Creator who guided Silvia Hartmann through the complex journey of her life to enrich so many of us.

For me EmoTrance is a wonderful confirmation of the personal love of our Creator for each of us today.

Margarita Foley, 2007
EmoTrance Practitioner and Trainer

EmoTrance In Action

In this section, you can read some personal experiences people have had with EmoTrance in their daily lives.

EmoTrance is definitely not just a therapy, but actually, a life skill that truly transforms the emotional experience of the world around us.

EmoTrance At The Dentist

I have had a great fear of dentists since my youth, when it still really used to hurt and there were no injections given to numb the pain. This got worse after being treated by a dentist who "drilled everything" for extra money and near enough ruined my teeth in the process in my early 20s; by the time I was 30, I would not go near a dentist unless the pain was excruciating, and then only if they gave me a Valium first.

So I got a toothache and it was no good - a dentist would have to be visited.

I treated the fears as they came up, mostly my stomach turning and my head hurting, which got me to make the appointment and into the office, into the chair on the day.

They made me lie back and that's when I really started to panic.

But this time, it occurred to me to ask myself, "Now where do I feel that massive fear and stress in my body?"

To my interest and also astonishment, it was a HUGE blockage all around my lower back, in the lumbar region, and not at all in the head or jaw where I would have thought it might be.

Whilst the dentist got busy out there, I set to relaxing this erea, softening and flowing things and that really caused a complete threshold shift all around.

Most notably, once that started flowing a bit, I became aware of the acute distress of the tissue in my lips and around my mouth, being stretched and forced and pulled repeatedly and also clamped with some metal thing, even though all of that was anaesthetised,

My attention went there and encouraged softening, not fighting it, becoming flexible and flowing with the stress put upon these ereas by the dentists machinations.

I called extra innocent energy to that place and strongly encouraged calm there, flexibility and gave support from my side to what was happening.

This was fascinating to do and completely occupied me, made the session pass very fast (surprisingly so!) and the end result of it was that I had virtually no discomfort at all following major three-root root drilling there once the anaesthetic wore off.

What I thought after the fact was that this was the total opposite of disassociation - instead of fleeing my poor suffering physicality and leaving it behind, I came to it to HELP it out in its moment of need and did whatever I could to make it easier.

That felt very RIGHT to be doing, a strangely loving experience, perhaps a hint of how it's supposed to be?

I would also say that this experience has revolutionised my attitude to the whole thing.

I will have to trust that the dentist knows what he's doing; there literally is NOTHING I can do other than get out of his way and let him get on with it. I do the best I can from my end as well and hopefully, things will turn out for the best that way all around.

I found it easy after this for the very first time ever to make another appointment and be accepting of these processes.

I don't think I'm afraid anymore.

Contributed by "Shelley"

Love For My Father

My aim was to have a loving, connected, affectionate relationship with my Dad. The problem was that in thinking of that, his energy coming towards me, I felt a hard lump in the solar plexus AND a BIG barrier in front of me to my right.

I felt the barrier to be about the awkwardness of physical expression with a male family member, due to rejecting some kind of sexual aspect and something else about my Dad's personality that made me cringe. I worked on softening and clearing the solar plexus. It was a very hard energy, which took a lot of softening.

Then we went to the barrier. It was all I could do to allow a tiny pin prick of a hole in the barrier to allow a tiny thread of this energy through and into me and through me. But it felt good.

I opened the hole a bit more and allowed a flow into my right shoulder and down my arm and right side of the body.

Oh, did it feel good. I finally dropped the barrier and very gently allowed more and more of this beautiful energy to flow into me until every part of me was full to the brim.

I felt, warm, I felt complete, I felt full, oh it was so good. I was moved to tears at the experience that I never felt ever in my life before. The energy of my father's love filling me.

I basked in the fullness of this beautiful gentle energy for sometime, as it flowed in to me and through me, before a soft gentle misty rainfall to start to cool and refresh me. When I came round, all I could feel was this fullness and completeness and had a big satisfied smile on my face.

I think about my Father now with a new warmth and loving feelings. There's no barrier now. No coldness. I still feel the fullness now as I write. I look forward to our new relationship building. I actually feel love for my father.

Contributed by "Heather"

4am Heart Expansion

My personal experience with EmoTrance has been wonderfully rewarding. The day following my initial phone session with my ETP I was the victim of a robbery: my car was broken into, and my purse, containing money, credit cards, check book, driver's license, automobile registration (and who knows what else) was stolen.

That night I awoke at about 4 in the morning feeling rotten.

I did EmoTrance on the spot and felt my heart go from feeling knotted and collapsed to feeling light, twinkly and expanded.

I fell back to sleep feeling peaceful and the next day I calmly went about setting things straight, without feeling victimized or resentful.

A few days later, in conference with my ETP, I had the opportunity to experience guided EmoTrance.

The ETP and I were discussing a chronic relationship problem of mine, and I said I felt "slimed around my heart." Following their gentle prompting, the slime around my heart changed to warm compassionate tears.

A few days later, I had the opportunity to speak with the person I'd felt slimed by, and amazingly, I still felt warmly compassionate and able to feel their love instead of their intrusiveness!

I am very excited and eagerly anticipating learning more about EmoTrance and becoming a practitioner myself.

Contributed by "Gloria"

The Energy Of Best Sellers

I was in town yesterday, waiting to be picked up and having concluded my business about ten minutes early. So I wandered into a book store and was faced with the "Top Ten Best-selling Softbacks" shelf which held innumerable copies of each one of the Bestsellers.

"Hm," thought I (who has dreadful contortions about the whole topic of writing, publishing, editors, etc etc etc), "I wonder what would happen if I sucked a bit of that Bestseller energy into my systems? Well, let's have a go."

So I went and pretended to be rather indecisive so as not to be removed by the security guards for strange behaviour in a public bookstore and just floated my hands over the No.1 books (a cooking book by The Naked Chef (!)) and did a bit of EmoTrance there. Fascinatingly, there was extreme shielding of many layers, many types and all sorts in between me and the whole display through which I had to fight my way first before a "door of perception" was established.

Face to face with the bestsellers, so to speak, was very strange. Cold, sharp energy. Very focussed. Very interesting. Very painful as it hit internal blockages with force (which would account for the past necessity of all those shields to keep it out). No gentle softening here, I just put up with the unpleasant sensations as it basically smashed through the various blockages in an entirely non-holistic fashion. Ouch. But then when it was all done, it ran clearly and I ended up feeling very focussed, very sharply aware of things around me.

Strangely, no thoughts about writing. Or books or anything like that. Nor any memory flashbacks, insights or anything else. Over 24 hours later, still nothing about books came along, so I'm beginning to think this whole deal never had anything to do with writing or books at all.

But that I must say is one of my very favourite things about EmoTrance all around. Things, it seems, are not at all what I always thought they were. Which gives me some hope of solving some seemingly insolvable puzzles.

Since then, I have noticed the following changes in my behaviour. Firstly, I find it difficult to recall even how I used to feel about publishers and "writing for markets" and "artistic integrity" and such. I remember I used to have problems with that, profoundly, but I don't feel like that anymore. I just write now!

Secondly, I noticed that anger, jealousy and bitterness at "more successful" (aka best-selling!) authors has completely disappeared. They are doing their thing, and I'm doing mine, and good luck to them is my attitude these days. As a piece of behavioural evidence, before that day I was spitting acid at the mere mention of "Harry Potter". After, I went to see the movie, enjoyed it tremendously to my surprise and then went on to read all the books with keen interest and admiration. I would make the comment that this particular energetic adjustment has done a lot to make my life nicer, more pleasant, more open and I am very, very glad I did it. I can only recommend to anyone who has real jealousy/anger problems on any achievement topic to have a go at this, it is an excellent piece of very welcome and long overdue changework.

Contributed by "Hazel"

EmoTrance Makes Housework Easier!

Forty five minutes was well spent time for a young lady who felt overwhelmed so much by the thought of doing housework she sat down, had a cigarette and felt bad. At the beginning of the ET process she realised there was a heaviness all over her body, this energy came out of both legs leaving her toes tingling, she was then aware that there was an area in her head which felt blocked, this was softened and it left, this happened three more times in different places in her head every time we introduced the thought of the housework until, finally, breakthrough, she was feeling happy and visualising herself cleaning in every room of the house, playing music and feeling good about doing it. An interesting point about this story is, she did feel really tired that evening but awoke early, feeling good and telling herself, get up, get on with it.

PERSONAL NOTE: This is my daughter, what a difference. My daughter does not have a house like a palace but she said the benefits are still in place she can motivate herself to do it happily. This did have a speeding up effect on her elimination system as well and she lost a couple of pounds in weight.

Contributed by "Sally"

Friendship Is ... Sharing Energy!

A friend called me this afternoon. I was really glad to hear his voice, get me out of repetition of work for a bit, and said, "Oh hi! How are you darling!"

Friend: Actually, I'm depressed.

Me: Oh! Do you want to give me a bit of that?

Friend <surprised>: Are you sure you want some?

Me: Well it's only energy and I could do with some right now.

Friend: Oh ok then - here goes ...

Me <gets a sensation of a deep grey wide ocean type of cold but very powerful energy washing through my entire body>

Friend & Me <sigh deeply and exactly in unison>

<a moment's silence>

Me: So, where are you? Do you want to come over for a coffee and a chat?

Friend:<very brightly> Oh that'll be great! Ten minutes ok for you?

So, and whilst waiting for my friend to arrive, I thought about many things. About the man in the movie Magnolia "who had all this love inside but just didn't know where to put it."

About the amazingness of someone saying, "I'm so sad," and another responding with, "Would you like to give me some of that sadness, lighten your burden?"

About the possibility that if people exchanged energies like that openly, might some folk then not have to wring that energy out of hearing animals scream, or other types of victims for their "sadistic" impulses.

About how cool it would be if I could say, "Oh I am so happy!" and instead of responding with an immediate dampener, someone would say back, "Oh dear, that's wonderful, can I share it please? Can I have some of your happy energy? I haven't been happy for years! I've quite forgotten even what it feels like!"

There is so much we can do and learn to do differently - it really sometimes takes my breath away.

Contributed by "Julian"

Even Sceptics Can Be Healers ...

 Has anyone else noticed a real noticeable increase in their "healing powers" since the onset of EmoTrance? And/or a serious attitude change to the whole thing since we did the "You are a healer" exercise at the training?

I found myself, much to my surprised horror, calmly offering someone who had had a tooth extracted two days ago which broke and had to be chiselled out of their back jaw and who'd been in agony since the Novocaine started to fade, some "healing".

Before I knew it, I was sitting next to them, feeling around near their jaw with my hand about a foot away and before I knew THAT, my hand had sharply flipped over so it was palm away from their face and I was drawing massive amounts of energy out of their jaw that raced up my arm and rushed all through my systems. At the same time, the person literally shouts, my God, what are you doing, this is an incredible feeling!

A part of me is standing like five foot away with eyebrows raised and arms crossed as "the other me" just as calmly and with quiet efficiency goes on to clear a very old blockage/shard higher up on the person's cheek, sort some channels in their throat, neck and back and then says, "There we are."

Person totally astonished, moving jaw from side to side, pain gone and also, long standing always present ear ache which I was (consciously) entirely unaware of.

Total time spent, about three minutes. No EmoTrance, just straight energy healing.

And that is not like me at all!

Contributed by "Gary"

Healing In The Realms Of The Psychics

I learned some Reiki healing a few years back and took the attunement (as did much of the population of the UK!) but never really used it other than for family and close friends and then only very occasionally - until the EmoTrance training weekend I had the kind of notion that healing was a lovely thing to be able to do for people but wasn't really "my thing".

That has changed for me personally big time. My first realisations here arrived during the lunch break on the first day when we were playing around, were trying something out on me and ended up doing "healing" on my knees (yes healing for sure - it felt very "healy" and fantastic!) and I, in return helped out one of the other participants with something around their shoulders...

I know a few tricks with acupressure, tui na, holding neuro vascular and lymphatic points etc which have helped friends and some clients out many times - these are things that I've always considered kind of mechanical/adjusting techniques - I am aware that when using these things now something's different - I'm getting more positive feedback and I can really feel things moving through my hands.

It was this that was on my mind when I wrote my EmoTrance review and made reference to my experience (see below):

"It took a little while for me to get going with EmoTrance. Although my very first tryout over the phone with an ETP has had far reaching repercussions in my life of the most positive and exciting kind, I wasn't consciously aware of them at first (i.e. the "you are a healer" experience). Now things are very different. By the end of day one on the training I was feeling things I thought I never could, by the end of day two I was feeling things I thought belonged to the realms of others - healers, psychics, mystics, and by the closing of day three... well, to be frank, I'm still processing here."

Contributed by "Rani"

EmoTrance - The Ultimate Challenge ...

... A Week in a Caravan with my Parents!

I begin my tale in the true tradition of family revelations "I love them dearly but..."

I have just returned from a "holiday" in France with my daughter and parents in their touring (i.e. small) caravan and spent a most interesting time playing with EmoTrance during the many and varied opportunities that such a dwelling and combination of personalities can manifest.

I've done it before, twice, they love taking my daughter out and they are most attentive to her and she really does enjoy it. I, however, find it a shifting mix of a break away from e-mails and work, the pleasure of seeing my little girl, have huge fun and horrific oppression!

It's a joke among my friends that I'm a good person to travel with – I take things like Swiss army knifes and torches, wet wipes and the like – the kinds of things that people mock you for taking and continually ask to borrow. On the last two visits I was sure to take EFT and diverting reading such as Project Sanctuary they were both essential to my survival.

This time I took EmoTrance too...

From feeling trapped amidst the waves of one of my father's "serious depressions" and instantly being transported to childhood times of walking on eggshells for days on end (done in about 2 minutes) to clearing a most uncomfortable pressure in my head when he did an emergency stop on a dual carriageway and reversed back to a turning he'd missed that my mother had pointed out to him well in advance (about 2 minutes again including aspects such as "he always talks to her like she's stupid" and "he never listens to anyone" and how this makes me feel since he's my Dad).

This one I really loved doing. How does/did it make me feel? Bloody frustrated are the words that spring to mind - he's arrogant, you can't tell him anything because he can't/won't listen and on it goes... But where do I feel it... such a huge pressure across my forehead and down my arms, my fists were actually clenched and I wasn't at all aware of this until I decided to do some EmoTrance right there and then and really take notice of how this affected me.

I'm 36 years old and have always felt tense around my father, for sure the degree of tensions varies greatly, from light hearted and affectionate exchanges where it is absolutely minimal to the strain of us being very different people with very different ideas to the overwhelming stress of being around him when he's suffering more than anyone else in the world - it's always been there and, no doubt, I've spent years with teeth and fists clenched, tension in my head and who knows where else.

Once again here I am seeing EmoTrance as the most profound tool for dealing with anything that comes our way in the here and now and, pause here to reflect on the vast healing potential, getting things moving that have been stuck for years.

So here I am back home unscathed and unscarred and not, as so many times in the past, feeling like I really deserve a good holiday after all I've been through!

I advise all travellers to update their checklists... passport... tickets... EmoTrance...!

Ananga Sivyer

Learning From My Child

Following the out of this world experiences at my first EmoTrance training, I was high as a kite and the very next day, when my three year old "little monster" came rushing into my bedroom at the break of dawn (!!) I sort of automatically dropped shields and reversed the usual resistance - you know, oh go away and leave me in peace! Especially first thing in the morning.

But I was not prepared for what happened when I did.

The energy charged from him into me and I burst out into tears immediately - how could I have ever rejected this being, this star? Oh good god, what have I been doing all these years thinking of him as a burden? I immediately started the EmoTrance process, and an emergency it was too because I really didn't want him to think he'd "made me cry" - poor darling!

We ended up cuddling in bed and I have never felt so close to him, so loving, and so totally energised by his presence - what a total difference to trying to hide under the blanket and trying to block him out.

I can only say that was a complete transformation for me in too many ways I can see.

I am so grateful that I was allowed to experience this. It would have been a miracle gift to just feel it the once but I can feel it all the time and it has raised me, made me into a much better mother, I feel better, happier in my own skin - thank you for EmoTrance. And that really doesn't convey what I really feel.

Contributed by "Stella"

Moving House Made Easy With EmoTrance

This is a story about moving house, letting go of a part of your life but it need not be a bereavement.

This lady had to leave the house she had raised her children in and move into a small flat and one of the things she simply could not take with her was a huge room full of books.

Many of these needed to be thrown away, others sorted into boxes to go to a charity shop, but none of this could be done because the lady was incapable of putting the books into the bags and boxes and stood crying instead.

So she phoned her EmoTrance Practitioner.

The ETP suggested that she did not need the physical books because she had read them all and to take whatever energy she needed from the books and make it her own, permanently.

So the lady started with the first one, allowing the energy from the book to go into her. It got stuck near her collarbone area and needed a little encouragement, but then flowed away freely and she found that she had no problems at all placing the book in the garbage bag as it had become simply paper and print and nothing beside.

Once the process had begun, it became faster until all the books were sorted successfully and the lady felt perfectly happy, calm, steady and energised.

She had also a third pile of books, those she would take with her because she still wanted them in some way - a thought that had not even occurred to her before.

Following this, the house move went perfectly well and there was virtually no bereavement or regret to the change in the days and weeks that followed.

Contributed by "Verity"

First Successful Complaint

My 12 year old son bought himself a computer game with his own pocket money. When he got it home, it didn't have a free special gift in it which had been promised in advertisements and which was the main reason for him buying the game in the first place.

He was distraught so I suggested he should go back to the shop to get it sorted out.

He didn't like that idea at all, saying that the shop owner would think he just wanted to get another of these valuable collector's items for free.

I suggested that he should try it; that he was a good customer there and he had never taken anything back maliciously before. But he was clearly too scared at the idea.

I asked him if he would allow me to show him one of my "weird tricks" and I was lucky that time because the gift meant a great deal to him and had wiped out his savings too, so he was motivated for once and grudgingly said, "Ok then but it'll never work."

The fear of going back to the shop was in his lower abdomen and it moved real quick and easy - zoom and out, just like that. I was surprised and even a bit jealous how easy he made it seem. I have to struggle to even start the process, I don't find it easy to feel where these emotions are kept.

Anyway, it took all of two minutes and he took a deep breath and said, I'm ready to go now. Worst that can happen is they just refuse to give me a new one.

I offered to take him in the car and wait outside for him (I believe in letting kids do these things for themselves, they need to learn to get along without us). He went in, upright and full of purpose. Eventually he emerged triumphantly. They had opened some more packages and found that all of them missed the special offer item from that particular box, so they opened another fresh box and those were ok. He got one of those, no problem.

Not only that, because he had saved them embarrassment from other customers, they even gave him a free gift for telling them about it.

A triumph of personal development, and a triumph for EmoTrance, I'd say. And - did I notice a look of new found respect for old Dad there in the car?!

Contributed by "Charles"

Singing On Stage

Most people are afraid of public speaking - I am terrified of public singing!

Or should I say I was terrified, until I went to the EmoTrance conference and found myself the guinea pig for a public demonstration. I was already shaking when I was making my way up on to the stage, and then looking down and seeing all these people looking back at me, I thought I was going to have a heart attack.

I was shaking, couldn't breathe at all, and sweat was just pouring from my palms and everywhere else as well. I don't remember too clearly what happened next, only two of the workshop leaders were there - but then there was a moment where it was like all the lights came on, and I could see everything, and I was *me* again! It was incredible. Later, someone else told me that there had been energy stuck in my chest and throat and after that had been released, I had started to laugh.

From then on, I remember everything. I actually sang a song and everyone clapped in time - it was brilliant, such a wonderful experience, something I will never ever forget.

Thank you EmoTrance!

Contributed by "Anna"

The Cranky Patient

I had the most amazing experience today. I work in a geriatric ward and learned EmoTrance because I saw a practitioner for a personal problem. The next day when I went back to work, something happened that I believe has changed me forever.

We have this old man, an ex-army colonel. He is 83 years old, doesn't have any relatives and cranky as hell, dying of cancer, waiting for a place in a hospice.

That lunchtime when I went to bring him his meal, he was obviously in severe pain and when I came in he broke down for a moment and made this tiny gesture with his hand, like he was saying, help me, when he couldn't say it if you know what I mean. He doesn't say please or thank you ever, when he's up for it he just barks orders and complains all the time, nothing is ever good enough and no-one likes him.

As I looked at him there in such pain I really felt the shields I made around me, thick as a glass wall all around me, more like a tower really where I was safe inside and I don't know what happened I just dropped it and let him come to me, let him touch me.

It was the most amazing thing. I went over and took his hand and looked into his eyes and it was like falling in love with him, with that old man but it wasn't sad, it wasn't like I had always thought it would hurt to care for them - it was completely different. It wasn't sad at all, it was - just amazing, that's the only word I have. Amazing and energising. He stared up at me and held my hand tightly and went very quiet, and then he said, "Thank you."

I have since changed the way I do almost everything and I have never been so fulfilled and satisfied doing my work with patients. This is awesome. I hope the day comes when everyone will learn EmoTrance.

Contributed by "Jenny"

The 58 Day Migraine VS EmoTrance

At the beginning of July I awoke in the night with a terrific headache. I took the customary painkillers to no avail. I went to work as usual and within an hour I walked out, unable to deal with this pain. This action is so unlike me. Later that day the pain was so bad my husband took me to the A&E department of our hospital. From then the medical treatment stepped into action. I attended A&E twice more. I visited my doctor and within ten days was sitting in front of the Consultant Neurologist.

The pain was ceaseless and debilitating. Doctors, more doctors, medication, I could not have had more attention. I was admitted to the Neuro Unit of a seriously competent hospital. More medication. And still the overwhelming pain. I was C.T. scanned and had a lumbar puncture. The staff were amazing but they did not know what was causing the pain.

When I was discharged the hospital suggested that alternative therapies might be helpful.

Whilst in hospital our house was burgled and both my husband's and my own cars were stolen. Could things get any worse?

During this time the pain was unrelenting. I found myself withdrawn, angry and tearful, and the pain continued. We paid for a scan to find some reason, some cause for this pain. The scan revealed nothing. The pain was there 24/7 and was beginning to change my personality and it was taking away my life. I am usually optimistic, cheerful, and dare I say humorous. All that was gone. Who was I? What had happened to my life? My friends and family searched for anything and everything to ease this pain. My husband was wonderfully supportive but he had lost his wife. He was at a loss as to what to do. The pain would not go away.

A friend of my daughter recommended that I call Sally Canning, I was at the end of my tether when I spoke to her answer machine. Sally called me back and even though it was Bank Holiday she made time to see me. My husband took me as I was not capable of driving, my concentration and strength had left me. Noise was horrendous and it was impossible to touch my head. I was weak and in pain when I arrived. I was optimistic with a degree of scepticism.

Sally asked me to identify the pain, and the associated feelings, and together, slowly, we proceeded. I had a strange and unusual feeling. What was it? I don't know. Then I sat up, I nodded, I shook my head. It didn't hurt! WOW, it didn't hurt! This was me – hearing the telephone hurt, my hair hurt, so much that I couldn't touch it or wash it and had it cut off. It didn't hurt! The tears came again, but this time for the most uplifting reason.

That hour and a half changed my life. I have started driving again, I have started to regain my stamina, I have a life.

I have been to see Sally again to release some of the emotions that this experience gave me. I have thrown the medication away, and I can see the good and beautiful things, which had become distant whilst wrapped in this pain. I still have twinges in my head but they are becoming weaker as I get stronger.

The doctors said "A migraine trapped in my head", I say a miracle.

Thank you Sally Canning.

And thank you for EmoTrance!

Mary Eaden Parker

Sally Canning, EmoTrance Trainer, Nottinghamshire, England
Tel: 01909 472 097 Web: http://www.innersolutions-uk.com

EmoTrance VS a REALLY Big Spider!

I had a fun experience tonight which might not have been such fun - if it hadn't been for EmoTrance to the rescue!

It is a fact that if you do ET a lot, you get A WHOLE LOT better at it, and then, when there's some form of crisis, it has a much better chance at springing into action automatically.

So, it's pretty late, 2am, and I'm deeply involved in writing something, far away, in a trance, when out of the corner of my eye I see this movement that shouldn't have been there.

I glance over - and there's this HUGE spider, but really HUGE, body easily the size of my thumbnail and the legs spanning as big as my hand, happily scampering over a stack of papers, near enough touching my left shoulder and on the way to climbing on my arm.

WHOA!

I'm not particularly scared of spiders but I jumped about 7 feet in an instance and shot across to the other side of the room before I had any chance of even thinking about it!

Even as I was crossing the room I felt this column of pure energy shooting up from my stomach and I just gave it a little extra flip as it burst through my throat - and I starting laughing uncontrollably, absolutely an energy release, and man, was I wired!

High adrenaline, but GOOD, really charged, tingling all over, absolutely what I would call a major "energised end state".

Wow.

Still laughing and tingling all over, I went back. switched on more lights, trapped the spider after a brief but intense struggle under a large glass bowl and put it out into the garden.

That felt *amazing*, really good and I was back at my desk without fear minutes later and working happily.

I really noticed that moment when the energy column hit my throat. I was glad that it just hesitated for a second then moved up and out in this wild rush which caused the laughter, because if that much energy at that high velocity would have been pushed back down again, that would certainly have been MOST unpleasant.

Cool stuff :-) and I'd say, me 1, Spider 0 on this occasion!

And Hurray! for EmoTrance :-)

Contributed by "Cindy"

No Need For Words

Sara, a 48 year old woman has been physically abused by her current husband as well as her former husband. Sara contacted me after having heard me speak about energy psychology almost a year earlier. Back then she commented at the end of my presentation that what I had lectured about for two and a half hours was very interesting but seemed to her to be too good to be true.

In the first session, we did some EFT. She was very unsure and nervous to begin with but the following days she slept a lot more than usually. After that she found herself energized in a way she never had encountered before.

At our next appointment we started with some informal chatter before we decided to get on to work with her emotional pain.

This time she had her current relationship in mind. So I just asked her if she had any particular event or thoughts that she liked to have help with. When she answered "I want to work on ..." I stopped her right there and asked her where in the body she felt something after having said just those few words.

For the next forty five minutes we used EmoTrance, straightforward, plain and simple, fresh off the shelf, with client feedback, of course.

Not a word about the painful event triggering her energy mind was uttered. She only used the feedback from the energies that were stuck and not in motion which she could perceive as physical sensations and I assisted her in doing the energy work with my energy hands. And soften and flow she did! After 30 minutes of energy work she felt an excruciating physical pain in her right calf. She almost screamed. Thirty seconds later it just shot out from her right foot.

Her thoughts no longer triggered anything whatsoever in her body mind that she could sense any longer.

I gently asked her if she needed something or anything after having done all this work.

After some hesitation she said that she actually felt an emptiness in her heart as if it needed to be filled with love. She asked me, "Can you get it from somewhere inside yourself or has it got to come from a source outside yourself?"

The answer was a lilac flower on a book shelf in front of her. There where no shields or anything else that stopped her from letting the energy she needed into her heart until she felt fine and her face was glowing with happiness.

Like many other times I had just witnessed how the energy mind carry reminders or scars that has been made in our souls but also its willingness to let it go once properly addressed and worked with.

The wordlessness of the energy mind's memory and the wordlessness of the EmoTrance work often leaves me speechless.

Kjell Forsberg, 2007
EmoTrance Trainer & AMT Trainer, Sweden
kontakt@eftsweden.se
+46 (0)411 52 70 30 & +46 (0) 708 48 72 60
www.eftsweden.se
www.centreforenergipsykologi.se

Panic Attacks Outside - An EmoTrance Telephone Consultation

I had worked with this client for a while on his feelings of panic and his fear of going outside with telephone consultations. He reported that he felt much better and could often help himself as well using the EmoTrance energy flowing. He also said that he gained mental and emotional strength and stability from the energy nutrition. When he started to feel out of control, drawing in energy from the sky, the sun, wind and rain, plants in the garden and so forth would strengthen him and give him a great sense of peace and relief. However, he was still extremely nervous about going outside.

We decided to do an EmoTrance session using his mobile phone so he could get dressed and leave the house and we could use EmoTrance in the real situation.

The client Dan (name has been changed) let a lot of energy flow out of his head and his hands before he was able to get his coat and his keys. On the threshold, there was a pressure in his chest and his stomach, which flowed away very nicely and then he could go out and lock the door behind him, which caused another small incident with energy disturbances around his mouth and throat.

As he started to walk towards the pre-defined target, a shop on the other side of the street on which he lived and perhaps a hundred yards away, I noticed his voice was becoming strained. I suggested that he should walk more slowly as it appeared that he was getting short of breath, something that he strongly associated with the onset of a full blown panic attack.

There was a resistance to slowing down in his legs, especially in the upper thighs which felt very hard and blocked up. On the conscious level, he said that since his panic attacks had started, he would try to run from point A to point B whilst holding his breath to get out of the situation as soon as possible and now realised that this was certainly not a good way to go about this, and even might have caused panic attacks to happen in the first place.

I asked him to stop, and we worked on the stuck energy in his legs. Once this was released which was very quick - perhaps 30 seconds or less - Dan said he felt much lighter and his breathing was much easier as well.

Dan felt now able to cross the road and that went well, but the energy blockage in the legs came back and he had to stop on the other side again to slow himself down. I thought it was interesting that the fact that his legs were not working properly immediately made him try to walk faster, which in turn would cause shortness of breath, which then would make him panic and feel he was completely unable to breathe.

But because it was always the same feeling in the same place, Dan managed to flow that away more and more quickly as he made his way down the road and towards the shop.

He could see that there were quite a few people in the shop which triggered off another feeling in the neck and chest area. This he noticed himself and dealt with immediately and without me having to do anything which I thought was a very good sign.

He entered the shop and purchased a newspaper as had been decided, then left the shop.

Looking towards his home across the street and down the street caused another reversal in his stomach to become apparent. He decided to sit down on a wall nearby so he could concentrate on that feeling which was, in his words, "The worst place of them all and where most of the trouble always starts."

We worked on the stomach area for about two or three minutes until a big blockage or disturbance was released and he reported a shift in how he was viewing everything around him, also he said the sounds of the street were different.

I wanted to make sure that we should take full advantage of this session so I suggested some frightening ideas that he had previously mentioned to me. He laughed at most of these but one caused a reaction of strong pressure on his chest - "Like squeezing the air out of my lungs."

We worked on that and it dissolved very quickly indeed, flowed away down his arms and that is where he took a deep sigh of relief and stood up to help the energy flow through the rest of his body.

After that he said that he wanted to end the telephone conversation and walk home by himself! He was very keen and excited about it. He said he wanted to find out if he could really feel as good as this by himself, and felt he needed to find out.

I said ok I'll stay by the phone, ring me when you get in.

A few minutes later, Dan called up. He was home and quite excited still about everything, especially about the moment when the stomach blockage had shifted, and the pressure on his lungs had gone.

I found out a week later that he had gone out again the same day to buy some bread and had called a friend on the phone who wasn't a therapist and didn't know what was going on just to chat on the way. He had a few moments where he felt "a bit wobbly" but overall was very pleased with this trip, and a number of others he had undertaken since then.

Dan is now practising EmoTrance at home as well on random thoughts that cause him to become stressed and has booked another telephone session, this time to go further into the town and deal with crowds and queues. He said he was looking forward to it when before it would have been a source of dread.

This is not an instant cure but Dan feels his progress after all these years where there was no progress at all in spite of so much therapy and other approaches has been remarkable.

He said that the greatest pleasure of EmoTrance is that he is learning so much about himself, that he doesn't have to deny the way he feels but instead can work with how it really is and improve it from there. Those things together with the energy nutrition have brought him relief, practical results in being able to go out again already and Dan feels strongly there is much more to come in the future.

I am just amazed at what EmoTrance can do, and what I can do for my clients now. I feel as though I have been given a whole new lease of life in my work, and I would strongly recommend

EmoTrance to any healer, no matter what school they are from. It is absolutely brilliant.

Katie Jacobi,
EmoTrance Distance Learning Student, 2007

Completing The Diamond Transformation

Here is an extraordinary case story about a moment of intense love, experienced 30 years ago, a moment which should have been an instant transformation of the person who experienced it but was not because they took the energy and "enfolded it within their heart", keeping it there as a keepsake of the best moment in their lives. And there, it remained and it stopped any further flow or experience of something similar or even better - ruining this person's life entirely in the process and keeping them stuck in the past. What happened when they understood that they must complete the process that was started all those years ago?

I know we probably know this about EmoTrance by now, but it is true that I was really blown away yesterday by doing this spontaneous treatment with someone on a - well, I guess you can call it a "super issue".

The life defining deal, the real big thing, over 30 years in the past and having spawned innumerable symptoms, related occurrences, formed life patterns, belief structures and values hierarchies, had the deepest possible tie ins with people and objects - a huge big deal in all.

Now, this "super issue" had at the core of it a massive Guiding Star and all the rest of the system grew around this, as is so often the case with such experiences and their aftermath and basically, the person in question had been holding on for dear life to this memory/energy from their end and had built their lives more or less like a shrine around this Guiding Star of having fallen in love that one time, with that one man, 30 years ago.

The idea turned up that they were weary to the bone of their role as the priest worshipping and tending that one experience all those years ago.

Yet they could not see a way out, even though they knew that they would be wasting the rest of their lives as they had been for the previous 30 years - unless they could allow this system to become liquid and to let it go at last.

Talk about resistance to the very idea! Wow. That was really something. The emotional responses and pleading, absolute refusal, just everything in full out reversal at the mere suggestion that this would be a good thing.

So I actively took this whole deal and switched it into the EmoTrance world view and here, what we had was not emotions and love and contortions and entanglements and constructs and feed back loops and memories and pain and suffering and stories and and and and, but instead, this total clarity and simplicity of an energy that they had enfolded and held in their heart.

Literally, held in their heart.

An energy that was so intense and so dense that it was hard as a diamond, and if anyone would try and remove this, the person would fear that their "heart was being torn from their chest".

Rightfully so, as the diamond energy had grown into the very structure of their energetic heart.

And in this view of clarity and logic, it was incontrovertible that this diamond energy represented a structural problem of great proportions; that it physically and practically **entirely blocked the flow of any kind of energy** through the heart; that the systems below and around were parched and atrophied for the lack of flowing, living energy; and even that this energy had **never done what it should have done** to the entirety of the system **because it did not complete its pathways** and did not ever complete the entirely positive and beneficial transformation to the energy body its movement through the system would have initiated.

From this viewpoint of clarity and logic, there was simply no doubt as to what had happened.

It wasn't a tragedy.

It wasn't a blessing.

It wasn't Karma and it wasn't God's will.

It wasn't all those contorted meanings or anything at all, it was simply there, cause and effect, with the pathways to what needed to be done laid out in crystal clarity for everyone to see, to understand, to appreciate.

There was no doubt at all as to what needed to be done, and no resistance at all to having it happen - it was so perfectly and so clearly the right thing to do, the **only** thing to do that the person spontaneously said with complete conviction, "The transformation has to be completed, the diamond energy must be allowed to move."

As the person began immediately and without **any hesitation** to soften the very outside layers and ingrown connections to have them rise like mist and begin their journey through the dust dry pathways and channels which had not been used for 30 years, I was watching them with a sense of amazement and awe.

This was the same person who had thought that they could not ever let go of this; that it was the only thing in this life for them and they could never ever, ever hope for anything better.

This was the same person who had virtually fought to the brink of death to protect the diamond energy in their heart from any intervention by any healer, psychologist, therapist, well meaning friend and from themselves, too.

This was the same person who now, after just **one look** at the clarity and logic of the energetic realities in their energy body was feeling the 30 year old diamond energy beginning to rush through the channels in their body, beginning to breathe faster and glow, trembling as the transformation which had begun all that time ago finally was allowed to be completed right in front of my eyes.

They were absolutely at a loss for words afterwards and so was I.

We were just sitting there, looking at each other and this strange sense of epiphany? rebirth? righting a wrong? holiness? was right there with us in the room and nothing needed to be said - what could you say to that?

I came away from that with a whole new found respect for the basic principles of ET and a whole new respect for how that simple switch into the viewpoint of energy and flow had simply side-stepped all the energetic injuries, all the emotional pain entanglements, all the beliefs and decisions, all the thought constructs designed to protect the status quo and to make some sense of it.

And in this place of clarity and logic, there was a compassion to be found that touched both the person and myself so intensely. This was not a cold and barren place bereft of feelings. On the contrary, this was a holy space, a space of awe that takes your breath away.

Now that's what I call energy healing.

Silvia Hartmann
16. 12. 2002

Experiencing your Body Universe through EmoTrance and Massage

Working as a massage therapist I meet a lot of people complaining about tension in their bodies. What most people tend to ask for is a "hard massage" and to "get rid of" the tensions and pains in their muscles.

When I work with them, what I often notice is that they have a hard time relaxing while receiving the massage. Their breath is constricted and they do not seem to be in contact with their bodies. It's like they let their body lie there on the massage bench like a heap of muscles and bones, while they keep on their normal thinking, planning and worrying, leaving it up to me to knead their knots out.

Sometimes I even have the feeling that being in contact with the body would be too painful for them. They have been neglecting both their physical, emotional and spiritual well being for such a long time that it would hurt to get down there and really notice it. The only way for them to get in contact at all with the body is through pain. I think that is why so many people ask for a "hard massage" and think that the golden rule for a good massage is "no pain, no gain".

Being trained as a massage therapist in healing massage as well as being an EmoTrance Trainer, I have a quite different view of things. I have experimented with combining EmoTrance and massage with very good results.

Instead of working hard with painful trigger points, in my experience, working with the emotions and underlying physical sensations of discomfort (such as tightness in the stomach, a lump in the throat, the worry or anxiety they experience) and letting that energy flow through the body and out (without needing to go into detail about what caused it and when and so on) is a much more effective, satisfying and long lasting experience of relaxation for the client. Not to mention how much better and healthier it is for the masseur, who otherwise has a very physically challenging job.

Massage works best when it is a cooperation between client and therapist. I am not there to fix the client, but to help them getting in contact with themselves. They have to feel it is their body and that they have the responsibility for it, and then I can be there to help them release what has been blocked and stiff.

To me, the first and foremost aim with a massage is to make people feel whole and in contact with themselves, beloved and seen. This can only be done if the masseur is reflecting this in her touch. Showing the client that their body is beloved and perfect, through loving strokes and just the right pressure, not too hard, not too soft.

Giving room for the underlying energetic tensions to soften and flow in order to get in contact with the physical body in a new way. Making a connection between body, emotions energy, heart and soul. Relaxing into being. A good massage makes you get in contact with well being and not just pain. A good massage leaves you feeling yourself deeply from both inside and outside, filling your body with your energy, making you feel good,

I would like to share a story, to show how EmoTrance can be used in combination with massage.

A client came to me, especially complaining about her stiff and sore neck, but also wanting a whole body massage. I started out massaging her neck while she was lying on her back, but it didn't really seem to want to soften very much. I continued with her legs, and then came to her back, noticing that she still, after about 30 minutes of massage, had not moved down into a relaxed state, but seemed to be somewhere outside her body. I asked her about this, and she confirmed that my feeling was right, she was still worrying and could not really receive the massage.

She also said she had suffered from a panic-attack during that day, and she was still feeling anxiety in her stomach, and that this drew her attention away from the massage.

I asked her if she wanted to let that sensation of anxiety out and she said yes. As I held my hand on her back, helping her to soften and flow the energy with my intention and soft strokes, and telling her to have the same intention of softening and flowing, it started to soften up and move up her chest.

Then it came to a blockage in her throat and after some attention also softened and flowed out of her mouth with the outbreath. We went through many layers of tension in her stomach, and got in contact with different emotions. Most of the energy flowed up and out through the mouth, while some wanted to flow down her legs and out through her feet. When she got very emotional, I again reminded her it is only an energy, and we can allow it to soften and flow out now.

During the process she got the insight that this old blockage in her stomach and throat had to do with her inability to express herself clearly. She works as a therapist, and is more used to and comfortable with expressing her understanding and compassionate qualities. Being in her power, expressing herself clearly, straightforward and sharply, expressing anger and irritation had always seemed more scary to her.

After having released all this energy, she now felt much more clear and relaxed, in contact with her power and safe to express it.

When the energy work felt finished, I continued the massage, and finished of with her neck. We could both feel, her from the inside and myself from the outside, that the muscles of her neck were much more relaxed now. It was very significant that as the energetic blockage in her throat had softened, the muscles had also been able to relax and soften.

She also felt at peace in her body now and had finally been able to let go of the anxiety. Now it was safe to be in her body again.

A very interesting side effect of the session was that it also had an impact on my expression. Obviously EmoTrance must have been running on auto pilot inside of me as well while I was helping my client, because the day after I made a phone call that I had been putting of for a long time.

I finally managed to tell that person some things about his behaviour that had been affecting me negatively for some time, and was able to do this without excusing myself or accusing him, but just clearly expressing how this had affected me.

So every client is an opportunity for getting more energy flow in your own system, once EmoTrance has become a habit!

I hope this short story will inspire you to go out there and try EmoTrance in combination with different body therapies.

EmoTrance is a great tool to experience the universe inside of you and to let yourself be amazed by your unique Body Universe!

Susann Forsberg

EmoTrance Trainer and Massage Therapist based in Sweden and Denmark. For trainings and consultations, please contact;

Website: www.EmoTrance.se e-mail: info@EmoTrance.se

Phone: 0046-411-527030 / 0046-709733947 / 0045-40755943

Simple EmoTrance Techniques

There are many different ways in which the easy, simple workings of EmoTrance can literally transform our daily experiences.

In this section, you can find some easy introduction patterns, and some other examples you can try out for yourself.

Many more patterns and techniques for working with EmoTrance are found in "Oceans Of Energy" - The Patterns & Techniques Of EmoTrance, Vol. 1, which we highly recommend.

Three Simple EmoTrance Exercises

Here are three easy exercises for you to try to get a feel for EmoTrance and what it can do for you.

Learning To Follow With Intention

1. Touch or have another touch you lightly with one fingertip on the arm or some other part of your body.
2. Have them lightly massage or tap the area.
3. Follow the touch as it travels through your system with your intention.
4. Repeat on different parts of your body until such touches flow instantly and smoothly.

Emotional Healing Exercise

1. Call up an old emotion you know well and which you can feel in your body.
2. Where do you feel this in your body? Show me with your hands.
3. Place your hands and your attention there and consider where this energy would want to go. Assist it in softening and beginning to flow through its rightful channels, whatever they may be, all the way through and out.
4. Re-call the original experience and repeat until it flows instantly and cleanly, and the original 'emotional pain' is no more.
5. You know the problem is truly healed when instead of pain you experience a pleasurable, charging sensation (the 'energised end state' - beyond mere symptom cessation).

Feasting On Energy

1. Find any object, person, plant, animal, landscape, music, work of art, weather, etc. and tune into its energy.
2. Drop any shields you might have to this 'incoming energy'.
3. Where do you feel it in your body?
4. Where does it need to go?
5. Assist in flowing it freely through its requisite channels, all the way through and out.

Practice makes perfect!

EmoTrance is best played with friends and it is supposed to be fun, so ENJOY playing in - the Oceans Of Energy!

Greeting The Day, Greeting The Night

This is a beautiful and very moving exercise that benefits you in many more ways than you might suspect just yet.

Do the exercise for a week and you will begin to know just how much support and sustenance there is for us - simply by virtue of being here, alive, on Planet Earth.

Greeting The Day

1. Step outside as soon as you have risen and open yourself to the World.

2. Take a moment to breathe deeply and then say, "Day, I greet you."

3. Allow this day - rainy or bright, cold or hot, no matter what - to come to you, to bring you its totally unique properties (for not one day is ever quite the same as the day before, nor all the days to follow).

4. State your intention to receive this unique energy into all your systems, and now pay attention to any physical responses you might be having to this enterprise. Any emotions, where are they localised? Place your hand there and soften the sensation, until the energy there runs clearly in all ways. Any sensations of pressure, discomfort, nervousness, any sensations of rejecting this day at all, localise them and make them run smoothly.

5. One more time, re-state the words, "Day, I greet you."

6. Remain with this for just a few moments, then thank the day for its unique lessons and energies on this occasion and step back inside and into your ordinary life.

Greeting The Night

1. When the night has fallen, step outside.

2. Take a moment to look around, to get into rapport with the night and become a little more still and a little more observant, and then say, "Night, I greet you."

3. As before, check yourself for any physiological sensations or emotions which might denote an underlying energy blockage that stops a true exchange of energies between you and the night on this occasion.

4. Especially, look for any "stuck" energy that might have accumulated during the day in your dealings in the hard and soften this, allowing the night to take away whatever is no longer needed, drawing all this up and into its endless self.

5. Allow this process to complete - it can be as swift as a thought, that is entirely up to you.

6. Give a sincere "Thank You" to the night for its assistance and its lessons and then return to your normal activities at this time.

These exercises take just a few moments of your time each day but in energetic terms, they are truly profound and most balancing, soothing, healing and energising.

You will notice that with even two or three repetitions, your ability to channel energy from the day and night increases dramatically as your systems and their pathways are becoming clearer and more efficient.

To begin with, you might strongly "take from the day" and "release to the night" but as time goes by you will find that indeed, for both the day and the night what is happening is a true circular exchange for you as each have their own unique lessons and energies to give, as well as assisting you in taking what is no longer needed.

It is a beautiful and very moving exercise that benefits you in many more ways than you might suspect just yet.

Do the exercise for a week and you will begin to know just how much relief, support and sustenance there is for us - simply by virtue of being here, alive, on Planet Earth.

Innocent Energy & Perfect Personal Healing

The idea to let energies "soften and flow" away is straightforward enough; energy must always flow and we only get into trouble when it becomes blocked or the pathways disrupted. One of the big challenges for beginners in EmoTrance is to hold their attention and to correctly encourage the energy to flow and find its natural exit points.

Here is a very simple way in which to get help from a related source – by doing EmoTrance in the shower.

1. Step into the shower and adjust the temperature until it is just right for you.

2. Let the water – innocent energy! - flow over you and as this is happening, become aware of any parts of your body that hold feelings that you need to release; or you could think of something that troubles you and notice where you feel this in your body.

3. Direct the warm water onto that place and give the "Soften and Flow!" instruction with your mind at the same time. Use gentle, circular movements of the water to help unlock the stuck energies and start the thawing process.

4. Use the warm water to help trace the channels all the way through and out. You will now begin to feel pleasant sensations and tingling as the energy begins to flow properly.

5. Think of the original issue again and repeat if necessary. You are looking to get an INSTANT, fast flow that feels pleasant.

6. When all flows freely, you can just enjoy yourself or repeat the process with something else until you feel totally relaxed and fully energized.

This is a great way to practise EmoTrance and at the same time, remove disturbances and blockages in your own energy system quickly, easily and profoundly.

The extra energy normally supplied by an EmoTrance Practitioner comes in this case directly from the warm water; it will keep you on track and further, this can help to remind you of how to do this in any situation where something has happened and a painful emotion arises.

Heart Healing

The "heart of energy" is the centre of our energy body and the true ruler of how we experience life, what we think, and what we do. All major human emotions are "cries from the heart" - joy, love, ecstasy just as well as sorrow, pain, anger and fear.

For 12,000 years or more, human beings have unsuccessfully tried to run their worlds via the mind and it has not worked to bring about a true emergence of Even Flow - a harmony of all in mind, body and spirit. Here is a very simple yet very profound technique for "Healing The Heart", a powerful tool for all who seek healing or are actively involved in human actualisation.

The Importance Of The Heart Of Energy

In ancient text, the "heart" is held to be the king of the energy system - the ruler.

Although I do not consider the energy systems a hierarchy, but view them as an interactive ecology, I also believe the energetic heart to be of central importance.

In my simple pyramid model of the human energy system, it is clearly the heart system which sets the experiences of a person - or in other words, if they feel pain, fear and sadness with all the corresponding effects on thoughts, beliefs, choices and actions; and let us not forget the toll this takes on the body directly and in second hand fashion through poisonous addictions and behaviours.

The heart system also provides the other kinds of emotional energies which likewise produce the opposite effect - joy, love, ecstasy, happiness, feeling at home and light, effortless, balanced.

Most importantly, the feedback from the heart systems sets the mental states for people. Simply put, if you are happy in yourself, you think positive, loving thoughts; you see opportunities everywhere and you have the enthusiasm and energy to do something with them.

The Importance Of SELF Healing

To me, it is of utmost importance to take the healing of our hearts into our own hands.

Let me explain just why I consider this so important.

You might well be familiar with the wonderful feeling of "being in love". The entire world looks as though it has been freshly washed and polished for you; rain clouds smile at you; gravity is much reduced, or so it seems.

You find a smile for every tramp, for every beggar and all your tasks seem so easy all of a sudden.

Being in love is indeed, a wonderful feeling.

Unfortunately, it is really easy to mistakenly attribute this state of being to another person or even, another entity, such as a prophet or spirit.

Because this particular person triggered the state of being in love, it seems logical that it was THEIR love which caused this wonderful feeling and being, but consider this.

How many rich people, for example, have been simply targeted by a ruthless trickster who didn't love them at all, but just pretended that they did?

And believed it, and as a result of this, danced off joyously, entirely happy, entirely in love?

No real love was ever given at all, and all that joy and happiness was entirely generated WITHIN the person themselves - the state of being in love was always theirs, and theirs alone.

It is such a shame that people don't know this, or if they do, don't really appreciate what that means. If they did, they could no longer be blackmailed by false gurus, tricksters and con men and women into having to pay for being allowed to feel loved. If they did, they would no longer be terrified that "this one person" might leave them one day, and with them, all that love would disappear, leaving them lost and broken, all alone.

Having a go at healing your own heart, as best as you can, sets you free from second parties and their attempts to manipulate you on the one hand, and on the other hand, makes sure that your heart receives true love at last, which is what it really needs to heal.

Although the false love of a trickster can make a person feel better for a time, or while they are under the spell of the trickster, as soon as the spell goes, the good feelings go as well.

When you address your own heart directly and give it your own love, you will be giving true healing love which is what your heart needed all along and you will be twice empowered by being both the giver as well as the receiver.

What Little I Have ...

I have said many times that our energy systems are not working as well as they could. The energy of "love" is something which is generated by the heart; so if someone's heart is broken, they will not be able to generate this energy as powerfully as would otherwise be the case.

Many people feel because of this that their healing might not be good enough or it might not work; or that they have to seek out a great healer so that these might do the work for them.

However, in the realms of energy it is not the quantity that counts, or the so called purity, or power, or anything like that. A prophet once said that one tear of a prostitute, honestly shed, was worth her salvation when the bowl of gold and diamonds from a rich man was nowhere near enough.

To give ALL you have to give is the key to heart healing. Whatever it is, however little or however much, whatever you have, if you give it freely and willingly and with all your heart, it will be powerful and it will begin the healing process in that instant.

If your heart is "broken" and ALL you have is 15%, then that ALL is ALL and as powerful as it could possibly be.

That is why your healing will be so effective and so powerful; and although as more of your heart's systems come on line, are restored, refreshed and re-energised your healing will become more powerful, it will always only be as effective as your will to give your all.

The Benefits Of Healing The Heart

Even if one was to consider the energy system of the heart in a strictly technical sense as the nuclear reactor at the very centre of our energy body, it would be immediately obvious that just about everything else depends on the state of function and the output of this reactor.

Personally, I believe that all the major human emotions are "cries from the heart" - joyful and terrified both, it matters not.

What does matter however is the power of human emotions to drive endeavour, totally control thought, absolutely impact the body and of course, entirely control behaviour.

For thousands of years, people have tried to control emotions, not to have them at all and to run the world and our affairs through the thought system.

It has blatantly failed, because the thought system is and was always only the "general" the true "king" - the heart.

It is the heart which gives the orders and the mind which tries to carry them out, and really it is as simple as that. Emotion overrides logic, every time and to try and cut out your heart leads to nothing but nonsense, misery, and enormous suffering in mind, body and spirit.

Heal the heart and the mind MUST follow suit. It cannot do any other. It is structurally impossible to feel vibrantly happy and to think suicide; to feel love and think hatred or revenge; to be joyous and think sad thoughts. Intelligence, insight and creativity are all at their very peak when there are mental states of clarity and connectedness, when everything flows cleanly and a person is absolutely grounded in their own selves, and in the here and now.

Dismantling The Self Constructs

Lastly, I would draw your attention to a further benefit of concentrating on the heart that I consider to be of supreme importance and impact on the quality of a persons life.

People "think" the most bizarre things about themselves. Whether they are having delusions of grandeur, or delusions of misery or whether they are wildly fluctuating between the two matters little; all of these delusions are thought-constructs and worth - nothing.

Yet, their churning and conflicting messages and motivations cause THE most intense problems to people on a long term basis; some settle with one kind of construct or another and this will functionally become their very own cage from which they will never be able to escape; others drive themselves insane vacillating between this and that from day to day, always at the mercy of a stranger's look or comment to send them into a spiral of misery, or on a brief and just as ill-fated journey of delight.

All these different self-constructs are nothing but fragile thought forms at the energetic level, and none of them actually have a true heart - only the REAL energy body has that.

By focussing on the one and only real heart, a stabilisation of the true self begins to occur. It becomes clearer and clearer and ever more powerfully apparent what is really the self - the true totality - and what was nothing but a half formed thought form, created from pain or confusion, as an accident, as a shield from fear or pain or simply because it was pushed on an individual from the outside.

By focussing on simply healing our hearts, we begin the process of getting to know ourselves again, to find out who we really are. What our true heart's desires are. What is real and what was always just an illusion.

Your Own Hands, Your Own Heart

So, I would offer you the simple heart healing meditation to try for yourself and find out for yourself what it can do for you. It takes no time at all and can be done for its own sake; indeed I would encourage you strongly to consider giving some attention to your heart of energy in the same way that you would remember to brush your teeth. Hearts go on when teeth have long become history, trust me, it is really worth it on so many levels, for so many reasons.

You can also use this very, very simple healing technique at any time you are sad, or frightened, and when you feel lonely.

It really doesn't matter why you feel the way you do, who it was that broke your heart or what happened in the past. When your heart is really healed, there will be no more history. You will be you and you will be new. In this spirit, this technique does not require any investigation and hardly any thought - just the will to healing and the gesture is quite enough.

Should you ever find yourself in a place where you cannot place your hands on your heart, it is equally effective to imagine the healing hands on your heart of energy, allowing your own energy system, who knows you the best and most intimately in all the world, do what must be done to help restore the Even Flow.

The Heart Healing Prayer

Simply follow the instructions given in the poem below.

You might like to repeat the poem as you place your hands on your own heart to help you focus your mind on healing the heart, and to get into the right attitude and state of being.

Hold the posture for as long as you want, or just a minute or two; when you are done for now, take a deep breath in and out and come back to ordinary awareness.

Please do not be deceived by the apparent simplicity of this method. The most powerfully effective principles in this world have a habit of being extremely simple, and the theory and practice of Heart Healing are an example of this.

Simple EmoTrance Techniques

I put my healing hands

On my heart of energy

To heal what once was broken

To make right what once went wrong

To soften and to flow

To restore the Even Flow

So that my heart of energy

can once again

shine like the sun.

More On Heart Healing:
* Download the Heart Healing Meditation mp3 FREE from
www.DragonRising.com
* Heart Healing & The HEROS system are described in detail in Living Energy
- The Patterns & Techniques Of EmoTrance Vol. 2

Filling The Void

"Since my husband died," the middle aged lady said to her friend in the queue for the checkout, "there has been such a void in my heart and I just don't know how to fill it ..."

This resonated with me strongly, especially the word, "void".

An absence, a hole, something that has gone missing, an erea of low pressure that pulls in on itself - and that hurts.

Do I have a void? Where do I feel that in my body?

Even as I thought it, my hands went to my stomach and I got a sense of something old, something that felt eternally hungry, unfulfilled.

Oooh ....

Now the checkout queue in ASDA isn't the best place in the world to deal with deep level, ancient energy body disturbances; so at that time, I sent some energy from my healing hands there to soothe it for now and made the decision to do something with that just as soon as I got home.

So I did.

The coat was barely off and the shopping still in the hallway, and I was in the magic room, tuning in to that old void again.

It really did feel so very, very old, as though I had always had that with me - I got a vague impression of a hungry baby, way past crying for food, with stomach cramps because the stomach was so empty.

When you work with yourself, you have to watch that sort of thing. The impression I got is interesting to be sure; it may even be absolutely true and the real source of that "void" I could feel now, near enough fifty years later, but to get into a train of thought, memory, accusations or feeling sorry for yourself isn't going to do a thing to finally and actually FILL THE VOID.

That requires to step back, take a deep breath and re-focus on the here and now; let all thoughts of neglected babies and whose fault that was drop away absolutely and to remember that NOW, all of that is ONLY existing in the energy matrix - it is ONLY AN ENERGY.

Where do I feel that void in my body?

I love the way my hands move without volition, on their own accord, guided by an intelligence that is so much more than my conscious self, knows such things, knows so much more than I do. That in and of itself is a wonderful thing - it shows and tells me both at the same time that my hands want me to be healed of this.

This thing isn't karma or self sabotage, and clearly my hands don't think that I deserve this; they wish to help, they wish to heal.

And all I have to do is to let that happen. To not get in the way with doubts or stray thoughts and keep my focus, that is all I can do, on my desire to right what once went wrong, to remember that this is only energy, and that my own healing hands have the power to do something about this - all I have to do is give permission, let it happen, and let it happen now.

Unusually, I begin to feel some energy flowing down from my head into my shoulders and neck; I say unusually because this feels warm, then hot. This energy flows down into my arms and hands and from there, into my stomach. I also notice further waves like hot water going down my back at the same time.

Then for no reason that I can discern, I start to cry. But that's alright, for that is also only an expression of an energy movement, I guess something is shifting and coming loose. This unusual warm energy is beginning to fill my stomach, makes it relax and relieves pressure and pain. I must remember to breathe deeply, not to lock up in concentration. As soon as I do that, the energy flow increases as does the sense of warmth, and comfort.

I keep breathing and think that I want this to be put to rights, re-establish the Even Flow there, make it good, make it right. The sensations are strangely pleasant, very soothing, so much so that I'm feeling tired now and sleepy. Just in time I catch that and think, ok, this is only an energy, I'm doing EmoTrance, this is not an energised end state yet. So I breathe deeply in and out to wake myself up and deliberately increase the flow of the energy to find the exit point for the system - there must be one, energy must flow in - AND OUT.

I am getting a sense that I have made a first connection to the "void system" by filling it, and now I'm looking for a second connection which will complete the circuit. How does this energy leave the space? What are the natural channels and pathways? I can feel a pressure near my coccyx and place my attention there for some "softening and flowing" - and there it is! As the energy finds its exit point and literally bursts out of the bottom of my spine, there is that fantastic sensation that heralds the beginning of the "energised end state"! At first, this is a huge relief - pressure released, deep breaths, oh yes, this is better!

Those who have experience of this will know that you're then in a strange, light headed, giddy state - smiling, wriggling, giggling with that energy flow, and electric sensations all over. It feels really, really good.

And the void?

No void. No pressure, no pain, just an overall feeling of lightness and brightness, HAPPINESS.

For a time, you're just too happy to sit still and you have to walk around, moving your arms, shoulders, neck and feet and as it calms down, thoughts come back.

I start reflecting on this experience and thinking about voids in general. This void I had, what kind of system that might be, how it had felt as though it was endlessly imploding back on itself. How when the hot energy came, it was unlike when you are drinking a hot drink and you can feel it sliding down your throat and into your stomach, creating a warming sensation, and whether I might have tried in the past to fill the void physically with hot drinks for that reason. And what other voids there might exist in me, or in other people, and how things would be different for me and them if they could handle that void thing with energy - which is probably the ONLY thing that can help for real in the long run.

And then I thought of the lady in the supermarket whose husband had died, and I spend the following time sending her my best wishes, and my best space time quantum healing efforts for her void.

A void is a strange thing. It is not so much as problem you think you have, but a solution that you don't - not an obvious burden, but some kind of anti-burden which is just as unhealthy in the long run.

So all you energy psychology enabled folk out there with problems that seem ELUSIVE, perhaps there might be some merit in looking in that direction and asking oneself, "Do I have a void in my life? And where do I feel that in my body?"

With the location established, EFT can help too by tapping on the void, the reasons for the void, and the sensations deriving from the void. Self help EmoTrance or to do this with a friend, or in a circle, is going to be a very interesting experience too.

The other thing is, I do believe voids can cause long term health problems just as serious in nature as blockages and injuries. And depending on where they are located, they can certainly cause what appear to be behaviour problems, or even life choice problems. If there is a void in your systems, you can't function properly and fixing that NOW is definitely prophylactic - and very energizing, very reconciling, and very relieving which I can tell you from experience.

As always, it will be most interesting to see what happens next, and what changes will come along as a result of "filling the void".

That is the fun part beyond the good feelings, and the knowledge that you have done a good deed in the spirit of the Even Flow on this day.

There are always "side effects" from these kinds of treatments. Sometimes they are immediately obvious, other times they present themselves as complete surprises - you find yourself thinking something or doing something you have never done before, didn't even think you could think or do, and sometimes, these things are experiences.

Apparently, Buddha said that the root of all misery is desire.

Perhaps the root of all desire are voids.

So let's fill them - and let's find out what happens next.

Wishing you fulfilments in their widest possible metaphorical sense, always.

Silvia Hartmann

Healing Hands Massage

... With Your Healing Hands Of Spirit

Healing Hands are the "hands of spirit" - your energy body or energy person has energy hands, and these healing hands of energy have the power to TOUCH the energy system of your own energy body, and that of other people.

Just as your flesh-and-bone hands can massage away hard blockages in muscles and cause a sigh of relaxation, your hands of spirit can massage away blockages in the energy system.

Blockages in the energy system, injuries and disturbances there lead firstly, to EMOTIONAL PAIN - that is the way our spirit person tells us when something is wrong.

When a person says, "I feel I have the weight of the world on my shoulders," for example, they are talking about a REAL FEELING of pressure on their neck and shoulders.

That is indicative of an energy blockage - the energy can't get in and so it is pushing, creating the very real sensation of a weight pressing down.

People have pressures on their heads, pains in their heart, weights in their legs and so much more beside, and all of that can't be cured with physical pushing but it needs your healing hands of energy to do the work.

"Switching On" Your Healing Hands

If you want to pick up a cup, you have to tell your hand to go and do that. If you don't, the hand will just hang there and do absolutely nothing.

That's the same with our healing hands of energy - unless you consciously switch them on and give them permission to go to work, they too will hang like the forgotten wings of an angel and nothing is happening at all.

So for a first simple exercise in switching on your energy hands which will do the energy healing when it comes to it, just for a moment now close your eyes and focus on your hands. Feel the sensations of your physical hands, you can rub them together lightly to remind yourself what that is like.

Now, widen your awareness and ask that your hands of energy should come into alignment with your physical hands, that they should be together and present at the same time, and that all the movements and intentions of your physical hands also translate into the movements of your healing hands - that both should come together now and act as one on this occasion.

Self Healing Hands!

Take a deep breath and put your awareness in your body, where your body is telling you that there are "feelings" that seem to have no physical origin.

For example, you might experience a tightness in the throat or in the jaw, but there is no-one and nothing in ACTUALITY who is wrapping their hands around your neck or holding on to your head - that's a "spirit sensation" that's telling us exactly WHERE we need to put our spirit hands to accomplish the healing.

Now, place your healing hands - the physical hands and the spirit hands together - on that place where you have these spirit sensations, close your eyes and make a healing intention.

Simply think to yourself, "Healing hands of mine, you are of energy, you know what to do, these are your realms, please heal this, heal it now, restore this system to the Even Flow as it was designed to be."

Take feedback from the sensations and keep focussed on healing, on putting now to rights what once went wrong, and trusting in the knowledge that your own healing hands of energy

WILL know exactly what to do - all YOU have to do is to keep the intention steady.

Giving Yourself A Healing Hands Massage

This is a fantastic way to practice with your healing hands of energy; to learn what you are doing and what it feels like when old energy blockages begin to release, start to soften and to flow away, and the pressure recedes and you are feeling better, so much lighter and that's such a wonderful relief.

It is also your incentive to do this often, do more of it; and very importantly, to become AWARE of your own "sensations of the spirit", so you can take action right away and you don't have to spend 30 years in emotional misery just because someone told you they don't love you anymore!

Remember to keep your focus on touching the energy system, your energy person, and that's somebody who has been neglected for a long time and who really HUNGERS for the love, the attention and the ENERGY your own healing hands can bring to them.

Giving Someone Else A Healing Hands Massage

A healing hands massage is by definition, a massage for the energy person. As you are not physically digging deep into someone's structure, this can be done by ANYONE AT ALL and you don't need ANY training for it at all - you just need to have your heart in the right place, and to WANT to help the spirit person of the person you will be touching.

Keep repeating to yourself as you let your healing hands lead the way that you simply want to restore the Even Flow, simply put things to rights - that's what healing is all about, and it's a wonderful thing for the recipient indeed.

If you wanted to, you could ask the person where it hurts the most; where the greatest "injuries of the spirit person" are located in their bodies; this is a wonderful thing to do and it also relieves you of the responsibility to "try and guess" what might be wrong.

For a healing hands massage, a person does not have to take their clothes off, nor do they have to lie down (although they can if that's what you or they want), because the energy person who is being treated exists on a non-physical level where clothes aren't a hindrance - your energy hands can reach them easily enough.

You don't even have to physically TOUCH the person to perform the healing hands massage; this is particularly valuable for sex abuse survivors, but also for many others who are scared or had very bad experiences with being touched.

Combining A Physical Massage With A Healing Hands Massage

For trained massage therapists, adding the FANTASTIC dimension of the healing hands at the same time as doing the normal physical massage is really nothing short of a revelation.

Here, you are combining the best of both worlds, and you are performing a ceremony of re-connection that is awesome in its power - and both for the massage therapist, as well as for the client.

See, when we have our healing hands and our physical hands in the same place and aligned in the intention to soothe and to heal, to restore the Even Flow BOTH in body AS WELL AS in the spirit, we're finally doing something very right, and something should have ALWAYS been like that to start with.

For the client, to have their spirit and their body called to the same place, at the same time, is - well it's awesome. It is what so many people have been waiting for SO long. It is something they might have NEVER experienced outside of a sexual relationship and they might have thought that that's the ONLY place you can feel so - BELOVED, so WHOLE, so HAPPY.

But that's how we should feel like all the time and as a matter of course! We should be walking around being there, our hands and bodies and our energy mind and all of us IN THE SAME PLACE, AT THE SAME TIME.

When that happens, that's happiness - that's the beginning of a REAL life for any human being at all.

It is an incredible thing, and any massage therapist who has the will to "help brighten spirits" can do so - simply for the asking, for the attention, for the knowledge about the workings of their own healing hands and without ever having to say a word about it to the client if they don't want to.

In the "healing hands massage", more than in any other form of human interaction, there exists the REAL convergence of the body, the mind (will) and the spirit, to bring that about, and easily so, joyfully so.

This is truly extraordinary healing, and I wish that EVERYONE would have the chance to experience this for themselves - as a healer, and as a one who receives the healing hands massage.

EmoTrance Innovations

Since its inception in 2002, EmoTrance has proven a wonderful tool for finding out more about the energy system, and how we work as human beings.

As the basic premises are straightforward and testable in experience, this has led to new research and specialist applications.

Here are just some examples of the latest developments in EmoTrance.

EmoTrance BeauTy T:
True Beauty Without Surgery

When you look into the mirror, what do you see?

Do you see your own true beauty?

Do you feel joyous, radiantly alive and entirely in love with your self in all the aspects, levels and layers?

This is not a rhetorical question, even though the answer for the vast majority of the human race is unfortunately, a resounding "No!"

With the crazy quest for everlasting "youth" through pills, potions and plastic surgery in full swing in the 1st Worlds today, there is the terror of the signs of aging - grey hair, wrinkles, age spots, saggy skin.

Stand before the mirror.

ARE YOU BEAUTIFUL?

"Beautiful?! You've got to be kidding me! Look at the state of me!"

That's one side of the coin.

But by all means, let us now go into any school where bright young things in the finest blossom of their very youth are congregating. Let us take a hundred 16 year olds from every gender, economic background, race, family background, and one by one, drag them in front of the crystal clear mirror and ask THEM the same question:

ARE YOU BEAUTIFUL?

You know what they will tell you. Many will even start to cry and beg to be allowed to leave the room with the big mirror because they can't stand the ugliness they perceive when they look in that direction.

Now let us take the final step and bring forth one hundred of the most highly acclaimed most beautiful people in the world, and stand them before that same mirror again, and now we ask these:

ARE YOU BEAUTIFUL?

And the answers will always be the same - my nose is too big, my lips are too small, my eyes are the wrong colour, my hair is awful, my breasts are too big/small/droopy/in the wrong position, I'm too fat, too skinny, too tall, too short, and it goes on and on and on ...

What on EARTH has happened to us all?

What is going on here?

And the question we must ask is, with EVERYONE to a man, woman, teenager, old lady and child alike thinks they are so HIDEOUSLY UGLY - and they don't just THINK this, they FEEL THIS, a deep pain that resides in the very centre of their being and it never goes away - then HOW ON EARTH are they ever going to expect to find true love? How can they love THEMSELVES which all and every school of psychology and religion holds to be the absolutely FUNDAMENTAL core of being able to do anything in this world at all?

How can they find respect, success, validation, JOY in life?

The very foundation upon which all of this is built is not just missing, it is inverted - perverted, you might even say.

How did this happen?

That's a long story and really and truly, for EmoTrance and in the context of starting to heal these incredibly deep and incredibly old injuries to the self concept - what the conscious mind THINKS the body and the person actually looks like, sounds like, moves like and what impression this makes on others! - it isn't necessary to know just how this happened, how literally billions of people end up thinking they are all ugly, on mass.

Look into the mirror.

Be brave, and really LOOK.

Where do you feel that disappointment, that sadness, that anger?

Where do you feel that in your body?

Show me with your hands where it hurts you the most.

THAT is where the prime injuries in your energy body reside; this is where energy flow has become disturbed, and with it, it disturbs our thinking and makes us feel the pain we do. It is not what we see in the mirror that is so painful - we are just triggering old, old disturbances that were simply never healed.

No talking in the world can convince a person who carries these injuries that they are in fact beautiful. A thousand lovers can stand in line and each one say with conviction this person is the most beautiful person they've ever seen, and it won't be believed. It doesn't go in. The channels through which this energy should run are disturbed and no longer functioning as they should.

But when we work with the energy system DIRECTLY, we can make a change there, we can make a difference.

And the most profound, the most basic and also the most far reaching difference anyone can make in their lives, they way they act, think and feel and how they appear to others is to heal the body image.

True beauty, a person that is glowing with life, has no age. This is not just a thing to say but it is true - beauty starts from the energy system out. It isn't a question of "what the body looks like" but a question of what the ENERGY BODY looks like. When it shines and radiates like a star, then a person has STAR QUALITY. This is extremely attractive to others who are drawn to this light; it is what makes others fall in love with you.

At the same time, it makes you feel like A MILLION DOLLARS. The functioning energy system is what gives us "energy" - what gives us life and love of life.

If there is only one thing for anyone involved in personal or spiritual development to really look at and deal with, it is the original body image and to strive to heal the injuries that reside there.

That is the most direct and powerful place, where the greatest changes can be made, and when they are made, the greatest benefits for a person begin to accrue.

EmoTrance BeauTy T is a specialist application of the general EmoTrance principles which focuses on restoring the "sleeping beauty", healing the divides between the mind, the energy body and the physical body, bringing literally a "fountain of youth" to a person and a totally different perspective on who they are, and what they can hope to achieve in this lifetime.

EmoTrance makes this not only possible, but actually easy and joyously delightful - both for the practitioner, as well as for the person who experiences the relief, release and then, the absolute delight of coming home to themselves, to their body, and to their TRUE BEAUTY, that will never leave them again.

Silvia Hartmann, 2004/2007

Energy Dancing

Energy Dancing is the latest technique set from the EmoTrance family - a self help program designed to significantly improve the flow of energy through the body. This results in feeling brighter, re-energized, de-stressed and to be able to think and act more positively.

Energy Dancing is simple, easy and uses natural, holistic body movements which makes it suitable for all ages, and for all levels of fitness.

Dr Hartmann, Creator of Energy Dancing and EmoTrance explains:

Energy Dancing - The NEW Breakthrough In Energy, Mind & Movement

"In a nutshell, Energy Dancing is EmoTrance with music. The Energy Dancing program teaches how to use rhythm, music and naturally emerging body movements to improve the flow of energy through the energy body. This is achieved by specifically targeting major blockages, shields, disturbances or reversals, and using the body movements, conscious attention as well as the energy flow from the rest of the body to heal and clear these types of blockages.

"When energy starts to flow again through these previously blocked channels and pathways, there is an immediate increase in overall sensations and feeling of well being. People literally come to life before your eyes. They smile, their skin glows and shows increased blood flow, and most of all, their movements become spontaneous and flexible - it is such a wonderful thing to be in the presence of.

"The Energy Dancing program is designed to teach this process as a LIFE SKILL, meaning that once a person has taken part in the program, they begin to understand what they need to do and what they need to pay attention to in order to keep the flow going.

"Energy Dancing and the skills set that goes with that sets up a feedback system so that a person can become aware that they are locking up, or that they are getting stressed, or that the energy system is really in need of some help.

"That's the first skill, to notice when your body and your energy body need attention.

"The second skill is then to be able to let very specific body movements arise which will unlock the system and allow energy to start flowing freely once more. This can often be as simple and easy as a few specific movements of the hands, shoulders or hips - and hey presto, an instant energy boost is the result as energy flows once more through the systems of the body.

"The lead in for Energy Dancing, as it is for all EmoTrance processes, are the feelings of the body. Whether these are emotional feelings such as being worn down, depressed, low, or vibrating with anxiety, or whether these are sensations of tightness in the head, neck and shoulders, heaviness in the legs, or burning in the feet and such, to pay attention to these places and to improve the energy flow into and through these systems brings immediate results and is very beneficial in so many different ways.

"What I find most exciting about Energy Dancing is that it is so easy - even with people who have never done any energy work before, immediate results are achieved. With people who know a bit about energy work, you get this huge outburst of joy and happiness because it makes such a lot of sense, and is so pleasant to do.

"It is a very natural, very holistic way of treating disturbances. Every part of us gets to take part in the healing mission. The conscious mind gets to pay attention and encourage the processes; the body gets to contribute; the energy mind springs into action to help heal disturbances and unblock pathways; and so for once, all of us is in the same place, having fun, having a healing experience, and learning something about energy as well!

"Energy Dancing is definitely the way forward to bring energy work to life - to make it personal, make it so that you can really feel it, feel the benefits of working with your energy body in this way. This program is a wonderful invitation to start moving in a whole new way - in a way that doesn't hurt, that doesn't exhaust us, that doesn't cause even more misery, like so many of the old fashioned health and fitness drills, but instead, that invites us to come forward, all of us, with the intention to heal, to get more out of life, to be healthy, and most of all, to be happy."

Dr Silvia Hartmann, Creator of EmoTrance & Energy Dancing

* For further information, reviews, complete program listings, information for trainers and free demonstration, please visit:
http://starfields.org/Energy_Dancing.htm

- *The complete program on 2 Audio CDs is available for £24.97 or £19.97 for the 16 Track Quality MP3 Library is available from:*
http://dragonrising.com/store/emotrance_energy_dancing/
- *For certified EmoTrance Practitioners, discounts apply.*

EmoTrance Relationships Consultant

New for 2009 is the launch of the professional EmoTrance Relationships Consultant qualification, which goes hand-in-hand with International EmoTrance Trainer Sandra Hillawi's new book called "The Love Clinic". This course and qualification is a brand new approach to the complex subject of relationships, made simple by the concept of energy flow.

The EmoTrance Relationshiop Consultant is an accredited training which lets you apply your EmoTrance skills to transform your relationships with yourself and others, as well as for creating more love, joy and connection.

Accredited by **The Sidereus Foundation** this course prepares you for helping people with a wide range of love and relationship problems.

This qualification includes:

- Energy dynamics in relationships for healing and transforming any encounter

- Blocks and barriers to love

- Overcoming old love trauma & Forgiveness made easy

- Why past highlight memories can be driving unwanted behaviours and how to release them

- Handling difficult behaviours and onto strength, compassion and wisdom to respond

- How to Increase Sexual Energy and release Barriers to intimacy and performance

- Energy dynamics of Love itself

- Relationship with yourself, towards greater love and acceptance

- Love Spirituality and Transformation

- Changing others and the world outside by changing within

- Getting Ready to Love again, Law of Attraction applied to Attracting the Perfect Partner

To become a certified EmoTrance Relationships Consultant, to expand your practice, to discover a new rewarding profession, or to simply enjoy a life changing workshop on love, visit the training events page for more information:

http://EmoTrance.com/events/

Learning EmoTrance

Here are some articles about EmoTrance trainings, and what you can expect when you decide to take part in an EmoTrance practitioner training.

EmoTrance trainings are conducted by real people – we have no "special gurus" with "special powers". You will find EmoTrance trainers in your local area, and these are wonderful, dedicated people who want to spread the joy and relief that is available to anyone who learns EmoTrance. Working together with others and taking part in the experiential exercises is truly fascinating; you learn such a lot about yourself and about how people really work. We say over and over again that EmoTrance is a LIFE SKILL, not only a therapy. Whether you are a health professional or "just a person", you will find that an EmoTrance practitioner training is a great gift and a marvellous experience that will absolutely enrich your life from the minute it starts, and for all the years to come after the training is finished. If you cannot attend a live training, the creator of EmoTrance has designed a special Distance Learning Course with extra exercises and full tutor support to make sure everyone gets the very best from the wonderful system that is EmoTrance.

Feeling The Power Of EmoTrance

By Sandra Hillawi

I had an email from a list member interested to come to the practitioner training in New York, but they were unsure if "EmoTrance would work for them".

I wanted to share my response as it brought up an important subject.

The problem was that this person could intuitively and intellectually understand EmoTrance and see its value, even see how it could integrate into their work, and was really drawn to it, but after many attempts still as yet had not managed to 'feel' EmoTrance for themselves.

This is what I wrote.

Your intuitive response is right. EmoTrance is natural simple and really only models how humans function in relation to their environment, and how they process energy, and what we can do about that.

I confess that at my own initial training I had a difficulty 'feeling' and doing EmoTrance myself. At first, all the triggers we were using I couldn't feel and everyone else in the room had energy flowing and spiralling out of their ears and hands. I thought I was in the wrong room with a bunch of new age crazies. I started to ask myself, 'What is wrong with me?' as I thought I couldn't feel anything, and then I felt this anxiety in my chest, a real physical pressure!

So that's what they mean about feeling emotions in your body! My hands went to that place automatically and I was able to have my first experience of EmoTrance and how it released that feeling of anxiety. It was amazing! And, not being anxious anymore, I became really excited about the training, and about EmoTrance - and that was a feeling too, a fantastic feeling of energy rushing around in my body, making me tingle, making me bright aware - it felt SO good!

Well that was over five years ago and What I discovered about myself on my own EmoTrance journey was that I was a very shielded person. 'Nothing touched me, and I was emotionally stable' ... literally because nothing was getting in, unless it was big enough.

After learning about energy shields and how to safely dismantle them I explored this to enormous benefit, for my reconnection to the world and my own personal healing. Further work on strengthening my heart energy has allowed me now to be a much more open and non-shielded person. So now I feel things!!!!! I can feel the beautiful things, the wonderful things AND the not so wonderful things - because even if it hurts, I also know what do about that. I am not afraid anymore of being open to the world.

After my own experience I seemed to attract quite a few clients with shields and helped them too, and got to learn a lot about energy outside the body in our wider energy field. If you know there's a problem but you can't feel it 'in your body' can often mean ... it's outside. If someone has had a lot of traumatic experiences or a chronic stress in a relationship, as a coping mechanism, there is often a conscious or unconscious decision to say 'Enough! I don't want this anymore!' and that is a pushing back of those energies which are causing us so much internal pain. But the problem is that disconnection energetically not only holds off the unwanted energies, but also a lot of other energies as well, so we become more 'numb'. No major lows, but no major highs either.

We feel 'empty' - because we are!

The world is full of energy and we need lots and lots of energy from everything around us to come in so we can be really healthy, and strong, and 'full of energy'. It is lonely hiding behind shields. It is a sad place that robs us of our joy of life, but it also robs others of US - we have nothing to give of ourselves if we have no energy.

EmoTrance is a wonderfully easy way to tune people back into a consciousness of how they function in the world emotionally and spiritually, to safely connect them back up to their own bodies and all the wonderful energies out there - and that is available to for you also. To go to a live EmoTrance training is a big investment I know, and I was in the same place making the investment 5 years ago without even any clue about what EmoTrance might be!!! I was drawn to it, I had only an intuitive feel about that this was something that could really help me. I took a chance and it paid off.

All I can say to you is, that if you do decide to come, come and say hi, and I will do what I can in the exercises to help you have the experience you need to show you that it can work for you too. I have taught EmoTrance to thousands of people now and it is wonderful - the surprise and amazement when they get it for the first time, and this whole new world of possibilities opens up for them, and it is all completely real!

Meanwhile, check out some of the traumas you have had or the stresses you have been under....and put your sensors outside your energy body and see what you can feel, check close and check far way. If you can sense something there, you are on the way. We can help you deal with the rest!

Fingers crossed that you decide to come. When you think of spending all that money....where do you feel that? Check inside and out and don't forget to check your head!!! People check from the neck down and forget the head is part of the body, and so many people store things in their head!!!

EmoTrance can literally do the world for your clients. It can make a world of difference to you in every way. Once you have experienced it once, it is there for you to use on anything - things you have wanted to do but you were unsure or afraid to try, things that seemed too hard or impossible - all that are only feelings of blockages in our energy system. You will get many times the investment back on every level, and even in financial terms as you can work smarter and have better ideas, without fears or blocks in the way but that's just the tip of the iceberg.

Any other questions or responses, please feel free to contact me.

Warm regards.

Sandra Hillawi

International EmoTrance Trainers Trainer

http://www.PassionForHealth.com

Live EmoTrance Training Experiences

by Silvia Hartmann

The following is an excerpt of a series of articles written by Dr Silvia Hartmann on an EmoTrance Practitioner Training, held in Germany in 2003.

EmoTrance Training - Day One

So, Monday morning dawned happily and I made my way to teach EmoTrance in German to a group of 32 people who ranged from those who hadn't even really heard of EFT, or TFT for that matter (!) to some who had specially flown in for this training and were pretty up to date with energy psychology already.

After what had happened on the preceding days at the conference and people's responses to my ideas and theory presentations, I was really looking forward to letting the participants interact with EmoTrance - that would tell its own story much, much better than anything I'd be talking about ever could.

I am entirely aware that you can't just read about EmoTrance and ever hope to begin to truly understand it.

You really do have to do it, FEEL IT, really experience what it does and how it affects you and your partners in the exercises in order to have some idea of what an interesting and expanding techniques set this actually is.

So, an EmoTrance practitioner training is a very, very practical thing, very experiential, and all the exercises are set up to directly teach the participants something that they will then know, totally integrate and always remember, because they have done it and now KNOW it rather than just to have heard about it and know ABOUT it.

The very first exercise in my original set-up (although not all ET trainers follow this for their own various reasons) is to play the "Insult Game" with a practice partner.

Hereby, one of the partners gets to choose an insult which has been a source of great pain for them and which is guaranteed to produce a strong physiological response that even a newbie at energy work can really feel in their body. Let's say as an example that for this person it would be, "You're stupid!", an unfortunate left-over from long gone school days and an "energetic injury" which has never been properly healed, and to this day, causes physical, visceral pain.

The person then coaches their partner in just how to throw that insult at them to get the maximum physical response; the partner does this, the kinaesthetic response is triggered and the most basic of all ET protocols then runs its course.

"Where do you feel this in your body? Show me with your hands!"

Now both partners know where the energetic injury is located and begin to focus on this, and as this is happening, both partners are learning about the pathways, the softening and flowing, the "it's only an energy" directive, and most importantly, they both get to learn what exactly happens when it all flows smoothly and the flip into the "energised end state" has occurred - when the injury has been repaired, the energy flows freely, and the former insult just creates a rush of energised, bright sensation that shoots in, through and out, causing an electrifying sensation and the person is laughing, clapping their hands and dancing with joy.

This is a simple and basic exercise which covers so many things and this group really went for it, throwing the insults with great gusto.

In a way, this group was great because they were so very innocent in working with the energy body directly; most of these people really didn't ever do much work with this kind of thing before and they were simply delighted how easy it was, and how good it felt.

Lots of people commented on how revolutionary a concept it was that one should feel so good and so alive afterwards; like most others, they were just used to looking for a cessation of pain into just "peace" or such and had not experienced that other dimension when it actually flips into the "My God, this just feels GREAT!!" scale which exists on the other side of peace.

After this first exercise, the group was excited, amazed, wanting to know more and rearing to go. The atmosphere was electric; people were so present now, fascinated and many of them had come to life quite literally during the first exercise.

In the question and answer session that followed, shields came up very strongly and rather than deferring this to a later date, I decided to go straight into shields because they were there with us, and set the group a whole new shields exercise which came to me on the spur of the moment.

Rather than trying to guess for something or hoping shields would come up on some topic naturally for everyone, I decided to simply go for something that each participant already KNEW they lacked connection to - just some topic, idea, thing, person, anything at all they felt as though there was a barrier between them and it.

Their practise partner would just stand by and help out as and when required as they together explored what shielding existed between the active partner and their topic of choice; I suggested they might try something like computers if they felt they had little or no connection to those, just as an example of what I meant by this.

One lady had decided she wanted to overcome her disconnection from "maps".

I couldn't help but raise both eyebrows at this and asked to explain it a little further, and she said that she just couldn't make any sense of maps - all kinds of maps, road maps for one thing, but also operating instructions when you have to build a cupboard or such, or even further, instructions for an exercise.

"Aha," I said, putting on my NLP hat for a moment, "so you mean **maps in their widest possible metaphorical sense**?"

She nodded seriously and so her set began. She said there was a shield between her and the "map" and she showed us with her hands. It was full body size, at least three hand spans thick and it made it impossible to read the symbols on the other side! (I couldn't help but think "dyslexia" ??? most strongly at that point - the energetic shield wavered and distorted what was behind it so it could not be **seen clearly**).

When she had gone through the routine of letting a little energy in to find injuries and disturbances which need to be repaired before a shield can be dissolved (and a considerable erea of injury had been found and restored near the centre of her body), she gave the command to dissolve the entire shield and just shouted out aloud, "Oh my, oh my, it's like roads, roads streaming into me! Blue roads!!!" and at the same time, I had the feeling I myself was standing under an electric shower, the shift was so strong and noticeable. At the very same time and before she had even started to shout about the blue roads, three or four people from other groups were turning around and looking over to her curiously - these people had felt HER energy shift all the way across the room! It was way, way cool and we hugged briefly and we both agreed that we didn't need to know what the "roads" were about but that it was just simply wonderful. I sent her off to walk in the garden and think her own thing for a while and went to observe further.

One practice team really, really made me laugh. The active partner felt very disconnected from their clients and had immediately seen that there was a big energy wall straight in front of them (a big shield) with the clients on the other side.

What was funny about this was that the helper was standing directly opposite them - and THEY were thus on the other side of that self same huge shield, and strangely (!!) were thus "not getting through" to their partner. I made them move and stand shoulder to shoulder with the active partner and boy, did that make a difference! First comment from the active partner, the owner of the shield was, "Oh I feel as though I have some support from someone else at last!" The helper could now understand the nature of the shield and help to dissolve it after the injuries had been repaired, and I thought how neat that was, and further, how often people are in such situations and not just in therapy. Perhaps just standing shoulder-to-shoulder with someone rather than facing them squarely on and running right into their existing shields can be a useful manoeuvre, whether you're an EmoTrance practitioner or not ...

Someone used the exercise to "drop shields" to a relative, another used it to re-connect themselves to the subject of numbers and mathematics and a truly fine and exciting time was had by all.

And of course, the basics of shield work had thoroughly been learned without anyone actually noticing this because they were way too caught up inside the unfoldment of the actual experiences.

Going back to that "dyslexia" idea with the lady who couldn't see the symbols of her maps properly because of the distortion of the shield, it was really noticeable in this large group that people used some key phrases which spontaneously turned up repeatedly. Now these people were very different in age, background, nationality and experience, yet they used the same words to describe their experiences. In this shields exercise for example, they said that "The colours became brighter, the lights seemed brighter" - "Everything looked sharper, more solid, was more clearly defined" - "Things became more 3 dimensional", and later on in the training, people commented that it was as though "people themselves became more real somehow".

It was truly exciting to me to see this in action and I really couldn't help but muse and wonder about disassociation in general, about people in particular feeling lonely behind their shields and being unable to connect to each other, simply because there are these shields in the way.

One further interesting note on the shields front. One participant did not have a classic Star Trek shield of a certain thickness and consistency but instead, the entire space in which his consciousness and the "other" existed was filled with mist, thick white mist which made it virtually impossible to make out any details about the other or how to relate to them. This participant also talked about being lost a lot, and being confused which this state of energetic occurrence would naturally engender. When this mist was cleared and they could "see clearly" again, a relationship with the other sprang into being quite naturally and this was an amazing moment to witness and to feel for me.

It is an extraordinary thing, in a way. Here I am inventing this stuff, I write it up and mostly forget about it then and move onto the next challenge. But to actually be there and EXPERIENCE people's responses to the various EmoTrance exercises was profoundly moving, and newly so each time I was a witness to this.

After the shields exercises and some more feedback and a little gentle reminder and wrap up session, there was a break and then it was time for abreaction city.

The fun thing is that we do the insults first and the **positive statements** much later in ET trainings because it is NOT the insults which cause people to burst out into tears on the spot, but actually when you tell them they are beautiful, or that they have a right to be here on this planet, or that you love them.

It is extraordinary but absolutely true that it is those kinds of statements, energies and the words which carry these energies which an individual has desperately longed to hear ALL their lives (but never did) show up the worst ereas of injuries and devastation in the energy body. EmoTrance newbies are given to arguing that it surely would be better to start with the positives and work round to the nasty negatives a bit later but anyone who has ever actually done this with clients or groups KNOWS that it is a very global thing indeed - a general occurrence and event for at least the 1st World Westerners we have in our trainings.

Love brings them to their knees like nothing else can.

Some brief glimpses of what happened during this exercise and which have staid with me.

I always instruct people in trainings to find a new and different practice partner each time, and to deliberately choose someone they might not normally be wanting to deal with, to extend their flexibility and to understand how very STRUCTURAL EmoTrance actually is. That it really doesn't matter if your partner is a small African lady or a big grim looking older man, as long as they're human and they really want to play, EmoTrance will work.

One lady therefore chose deliberately to pair herself up for this exercise with a second lady she didn't know, but who had deeply annoyed her earlier in the morning by her conduct in the restaurant. This second lady had not even noticed her there because she had been "bitching at the checkout person" for some considerable time and the first was just behind her in the queue.

So imagine her surprise when the second lady, the one who had bitched in the cafeteria, expressed her desire for her practice partner to say to her, "You are a really likeable person!"

It was not until AFTER the work was completed that the practice partner revealed herself and they got on really well and between them made some superb magic on that day. Ah, energy, synchronicity, being in the right place at the right time - it's wonderful, really, when you just sit back and look at it!

I saw a pair working on having a lady accept "You are the most attractive woman I have ever seen!" and once again, shivers went all through me as I watched and felt them do it.

A gentleman who had asked for, "You are a good teacher." ended up curled up on the floor and had to be lovingly helped by two partners to straighten out his energy system. Following the intervention he had finally some colour to his face - he had looked like a ghost, pale and drawn, all the time before and it was wonderful to observe the change.

This reminds me of something else I noted time and time again – namely that people actually and literally "came to life" during these exercises. Before, they stood pale and still, rigid throughout, and after, there was high colour in their faces, and there was MOVEMENT in their bodies, necks, feet, faces - wonderful! And highly noticeable, of course, to everyone who was watching. We didn't have to "trust our intuition" or hope for the best, you could really SEE and FEEL how increased energy flow throughout the energy body really wakes folk up, gives them a spark, gives them new energy and makes them so much more lively and alive. And that is infectious. Even I couldn't help but do little dances and hug people now and then, and that is saying something about me ...

We did a couple more exercises and people had now begun to get the hang of it. They were no longer talking about heart chakras or trying to re-phrase or lead the interventions; they were beginning to do this new thing rather than what they had come with and that was great as well to see as the day progressed. It was an indication to me that they were beginning to trust the underlying processes.

So with a very happy group and a blown-away presenter, we went into the evening fun activities before the second and last day of this extraordinary training.

EmoTrance Training - Day Two

The morning of the second day, I had decided to make a point of the fact that in EmoTrance, *everything* is really and truly, JUST AN ENERGY. That I'm not joking when I say this; that when I talk about emotional energies being simply injuries in the energy body this actually encompasses all and everything under the topic, no matter how horrendous, how old, how hard or how painful it was or still is.

For this purpose, I chose two exercises, namely "The Deepest, Darkest Secret" and "The Oldest Burden".

EmoTrance can be run with "content unknown".

This means that the partner, helper or practitioner need not know what the topic of the intervention or problem is; imagine this as the equivalent of someone coming to the doctor's with a big hole in their stomach, and it is not really relevant how that got to be there, or who actually took a chunk out of this person, or whether it was the person's own fault that they now have this injury and so on and so forth - what I tend to say is that, "We're dealing with these energetic injuries like you would deal with a hole in a sock. Look, there's a sock. It's got a hole in it. We mend it. End of story."

This is a very, very essential component of EmoTrance and what that does is to take both the practitioner and the owner of the injury into this other mindspace where things are clear and logical and incredibly easy to resolve, because you just don't get involved with what it means, whether it is a karma thing, what the lessons are, whose fault it is, how horrible it all is and so on and so forth which kept people in therapy for a lifetime.

So, and to demonstrate these three components, namely:

1. No-one ever needs to know where the injury came from or "what it means" (content unknown) and the problem can be perfectly well resolved in all ways;

2. We don't need to talk **about the problem** in order to resolve the problem (clear mind space of simple structural repair work); and

3. It doesn't matter how "bad" something is or how old, it is ONLY AN ENERGY and energy can be moved with consciousness in quantum time, easily, and just for the asking.

... I chose the "Deepest, Darkest Secret".

On the Heart Healing HD album, there is a journey/process in which one gives things one doesn't need to carry any longer to the universal ocean, and the words are:

"The ocean is enormous,
and it will with gladness
take all you have to give -
even your deepest,
darkest secrets,
those things you thought
could never be revealed,
you could not tell another or yourself,
and which pressed
the breath from your lungs,
and the bright star of hope
from your eyes."
(excerpt from Ocean Wood - Heart Healing HD2)

In EmoTrance, we really do return things to the ubiquitous universal "oceans of energy" and they are indeed enormous and will gladly take all you have to give to it. Further, carrying secrets in the energy body is one of those things I've noted which can and do cause the most horrendous disturbances; to release these is a huge, huge relief all around and a necessary pre-curser for love of life and joy, returned.

When the group came back from this exercise, they were different.

Quieter, much more thoughtful. I think what happened was that they were beginning to appreciate the depth and power of working with energy in this way; the day before we did have a lot of good fun and there, it seems to be this easy, happy little thing, but this exercise and the one to follow, "The Oldest Burden", really do show up how very structural EmoTrance is and that there is, in short, no problem at all that is too hard, too heavy or immune to this way of working.

I understand that this makes one rather thoughtful as a great many ideas one might have had about healing and even about oneself and what it takes to heal or to make changes has been so very practically challenged - and proven to be faulty in one's own personal experience.

For the "oldest burden" exercise I have a story which really did amaze me. The day before, one of the participants asked if they could have a word with me and they told me the following (all details have been changed for confidentiality).

This gentleman had a son who had died of AIDS some two years previously. The son had been 21 years old when this happened, and the gentleman in question, let's call him Tony, was in a process of systemic collapse. His energy system was folding in on itself; that's the best I can describe it; and the symptoms and occurrences he told me about reminded me strongly of what has been observed in "The Dying Process", a paper written by a hospice nurse to explain what happens in very regular and systemic stages when a person is in a hospice and dying.

Tony's energy system was dying.

In his quest to help his son, Tony had gone, like so many before him, to the end of the available allopathic remedies and treatments, and then in desperation turned to the holistic and esoteric fields of human healing because there was nothing else left to do.

This is why he was at this energy therapies conference; this is why he now was sitting in a cafe with me and telling me these things, how he couldn't sleep anymore, had no energy left for his wife, his other children, his clients at work, and how he had these terrible stabbing pains in the area of his testicles which would spread all through his abdomen and were so excruciating that he was then literally on the floor, crying out in pain.

Needless to say, the doctors couldn't find "anything wrong" physically and had now referred him to a psychiatrist; he told me that he knew full well that it wasn't physical, but he had to go through the motions for his wife's sake who was of course terribly upset too and after losing the son, was terrified she was going to lose him as well. He further told me that he thought the son had died "on his behalf", that he had died instead of Tony himself, in his place.

I did what I could for him in the cafe and now, back in the training, the participants are doing "The Oldest Burden" exercise and there is Tony, as I'm making the rounds, and his two practice partners, a very young lady who is a massage therapy student and a nice older lady, who is a kinesiologist, neither having any form of advanced psychology knowledge or experience, working on his abdominal area.

"Bloody hell," I thought, "He's really done it - he's really given them THAT for this exercise! Wow!" and so I went over to the group and asked the older lady who was the "observer" in the team at that time, "Well, how's it going?"

She looked up from her notepad, smiled brightly and said all cheerfully, "Oooh, that was a bit of a tricky one, but it's getting there - halfway up the stomach now, it's starting to flow!"

And I thought, "And you have NO IDEA of the severity of what that was, what that was about, and thank the Lord you didn't because if you did, you would have been - well, probably petrified would be a good word for it!"

I made a point of having a quick word with Tony in the next available break, and what he said was this: "Something unlocked today, something - unhooked and it has changed. I feel hope for the first time - oh, since long before my son died. Hope that there is some reason for being here, and hope that I can now turn this around. Do something useful so that he didn't die for nothing."

Personally I am not given to making any predictions or promises of healing; I don't even allow myself to consider that, not in my work nor with myself, but if there was any hope at all for Tony to make it to 80 years of age then I would have thought that working this directly with the energy body, resolving these things from the energy body up like we do, is about the most gentle and best bet we have at this time, and that was worth a lot to me.

Re-Defining Psychosomatic Disease

As a result of this, I also told the group when we came back from these exercises and the much needed breaks afterwards, that I would like to officially announce that I am no longer going to use the phrase or concept of psychosomatic or neurosomatic illness, but that I consider these to be simply emotions now, and that would bring those kind of "physical pains without a seemingly physical origin" right into the brief of EmoTrance treatments.

I believe that this re-definition of psychosomatics as being simply the highest end class of emotions will not just help those who are treating these to have a much clearer idea of what they are dealing with, and HOW to deal with these, at that, but also that people who are experiencing the pain of these high end emotions can then understand THEMSELVES better and no longer need to feel that they are mad, or having some sort of aberration going on there.

This is particularly important to me.

Feeling intense and disabling pain in the absence of a physical cause is thereby strictly systemic, normal and absolutely what one would expect with the highest end injuries in the energy system and how these warning signals progress if left untreated.

Size and State Of The Human Energy System

I would like to return now briefly to my observation about Tony and that his energy system was "collapsing in on itself" as well as my noting that his processes were remarkably similar, if not the same, as what had been observed by the hospice nurse in "The Dying Process".

A set of exercise which are amongst my favourites in EmoTrance revolve around the concept as how you can turn those miserable things I've never liked, namely "affirmations", into a powerful "evocation" of that form of energy or change which is required.

Very simply put, if someone believes themselves to be unlovable, and they look into a mirror and say, "I am lovable", they're not doing themselves any good but instead, experience emotional pain AGAIN - because the reason they thought that they were unlovable in the first place is most likely a blockage or energetic injury somewhere in their systems and when something of the right frequency (such as an affirmation!) hits that injury, IT HURTS SOME MORE and really, doesn't do any good at all. Very rarely and entirely by accident, SOME affirmations work but the majority of them don't, or at least not until and unless some serious other work has been done somehow else; rest of the time, it causes even more pain and depression. I'd been observing this for 20 years and more and got the point where when someone said, "Affirmation" I would spit fire in response, instantly.

With EmoTrance what you do is to say or evoke the energy form you want, for example, "I am a superb lover." Then you note where that HURTS when you say it aloud or even think it; you heal that, and then you when you say it again and those energies rush through and out clearly, you really get a sense of what it was that you were trying to evoke and you FEEL the shift, feel the difference the evocation has created with you and for you.

This group decided mostly to do animals for this exercise - shamanic energy evocation of the ESSENCE of an eagle, a tiger, an elephant, a dolphin and so forth.

This is a little unusual for this exercise; I think someone started with animals and then everyone else thought, yeah that's cool, I always wanted to evoke "the stallion within" and did the same; but I was really glad it happened because there was a very, very interesting aspect to this I became aware of after the third person said exactly the same thing.

They all reported that their energy field *expanded massively* when they tuned into being these animals.

For example:

"I decided to evoke being an eagle. I had a blockage in my throat and then found another near the top of my stomach. When that dissolved, my vision became sharper and I could feel myself expanding hugely, I had this sense of being so big and so high, so very powerful."

Or this one:

"I used, I am an elephant. I was really surprised, I always thought elephants were kind of lumbering and slow. But wow, when I had cleared a blockage in my head and neck, I felt this amazing sense of expansion, and physical power - I felt so strong and so alive!"

Now, eagles are considerably SMALLER than human beings, so why would the experience of an eagle's energy system lead a person to feel their energy field expanding?

Unless - people's energy systems are drawn in unnaturally?

Unless - and this was indeed a very frightening thought! - they are also in that process of structural collapse that I had observed in Tony?!

Not as fast or catastrophic as in his case, but actually and practically, doing the "dying process" over a longer period of time? Might that lead to the proverbial "grey men, leading lives of quiet desperation"?

I was most intrigued by that thought and what it also did was to bring to the fore once more how IMPORTANT working with the energy system directly might be for long term health and longevity even, if you want.

It may well be so that even we who are working with the human energy systems every day are still really seriously underestimating the importance of it as the very BASIS FOR HUMAN LIFE altogether. That we still may live in the old construct entrainments where there never was such a thing as an energy system, or that playing around with that said energy system is something you do "after all else has failed", if you have nothing better to do or if you're bored at the weekend.

It is certainly a fascinating supposition and one that would behoove us all to take a good long look at; and especially in the context of what one might DO in order to reverse this slow collapse and put things to rights.

The Afternoon Exercises

Now it was time for some new techniques, working with energy systems that are basically outside the skin barrier and thereby, perceived slightly differently.

For a basic and first introduction to working with ereas outside the physical body, I choose the Rainbow Connection, an energetic polarity/parts integration device that has simply wonderfully noticeable effects on people's physicalities, their states and their conscious awareness/thought.

Then I introduced "The Shadow" exercise.

Hereby what we do is to take a "something" that exists in the energy field and of which its owner has been entirely aware for a long time, possibly their entire conscious lives, and which is functionally a major disturbance in the wider energy field, hence the name, "The Shadow". We call all "somethings" in the energy system an EXISTING ENERGETIC REALITY or EREA for short; this is a nice structural term which isn't emotionally charged and allows both the owners of the ereas as well as the practitioners to deal with them exactly like we deal with all energy forms in EmoTrance - it must flow, it must need to go somewhere, and once we let such ereas find their natural pathways, they cease to be a problem.

One lady I observed had a life-long problem with something that turned out to be a permission issue - it was as though there were parts in her energy system where she was not allowed to go, or know about, or have contact with. This was a most profoundly interesting experience and the lady in question was literally (and very physically!) reeling as she needed to find a whole new balance all around. When she did, I can only say that I was most impressed with the changes, indeed.

I also gave the group as a bonus and gift from me to them for all their honest attention and hard work over the two days a short overview of Project Energy, a true multi-purpose energetic alignment device for use in business, family therapy and other systems where more than one component needs to be working and function within a "group flow system". They enjoyed this quite a bit, as I did talking about this - it's one of my favourite patterns of 2003 (so far :-) and very, very magical.

I also made a quick mention of Thought Flow, and then invited the group to join me for a Heart Healing session.

This was very interesting. As you probably know, I'm a General Semanticist and also a long term NLPer and hypnotist, so as soon as I started on the words to the basic Heart Healing invocation in German I became aware that I wasn't doing this right to be speaking it TO them; what would have happened was that they would have gone away thinking that *I* was healing their hearts!

This of course leads to the totally wrong conclusions and also, "Guru disturbances" of which I am acutely aware and highly allergic to; so I stopped everything immediately and explained that the core, very deepest core of what I do is to bring people online so they get to step into THEIR OWN HEALING POWERS and use those to grow stronger from within THEMSELVES, rather than leaving this to another outside of themselves.

So, instead, what I did was to speak a single line, and then having the group repeat the single line in the Heart Healing posture, much like you would do on an oath or pledge of allegiance. That gave me the time to phrase it right and to make sure that the right ENERGY AND INTENTION was present.

I don't remember the exact words and of course, they were in German, but it went something like this:

(I hold out my hands, palms up.)
These are MY healing hands.
(Group repeats gestures and words - each person says:
"These are MY healing hands." aloud.)
I place MY OWN healing hands
on MY OWN dear heart.
With all my love,
it is my full intention
to make right what once went wrong,
to make whole what once was broken,
with all my love and all my power,
I nourish and awaken
my dear beloved heart.

That was absolutely amazing, absolutely magical as the group spoke these words and the energy in the room was just totally wonderful, is all I can say. Holy, even, and in this format it was right - all these people there and each was an individual, adding their own individuality to the time and place, and knew they were.

I was most satisfied with this and so, we finished up with a Q&A session, and the training was indeed, complete.

Thoughts and Further Developments

To teach EmoTrance to a diverse group of people, many of whom had absolutely no experience whatsoever in energy work, was an eye opening experience.

EmoTrance is a superb system from every angle

EmoTrance is gentle and a whole new experience for practitioners and for the clients alike and it allows one to tackle the very worst disturbances swiftly and with confidence, even if one has no training in existing therapy forms at all. As you are working with what the client experiences and you are not guessing or hallucinating, you simply can't go wrong with it.

EmoTrance fits like a glove with just about every imaginable form of therapy and counselling, from kinesiology to massage therapy, hypnosis and NLP to psychology, reflexology to aromatherapy and can be as easy as saying a few words to the client to start the process.

EmoTrance gives you tremendous confidence as the therapist or healer and you learn stacks about people as you're paying attention to each client's unfoldments in total safety because the client themselves are in control all the way through.

For clients, it is finally a way to deal with things one has been afraid of and suffering from for such a long time; things one might have thought could never possibly be resolved, or would have to hurt as much again if one was to turn one's attention there; and for people like me who have been severely abused the idea of retaining full control over the processes yet to be supported by another in this totally respectful and gentle manner is nothing short of a Godsend.

I can't just lie there and let people prod my energy system to their heart's content, all of me goes simply on flat out red alert and so I have avoided this scenario all my life. With this way of working, I'm in control and can call halt to things if I'm getting scared and I get not only to decide exactly what we're working on and in which order, but also the ONLY feedback mechanism are MY feelings and experiences and what *I* say - no-one is telling me any more what's wrong with me, nor how THEY are going to put this right by a quick prod here and a quick prod there.

Further, for the very worst stuff I don't have to tell anyone at all what it was and where it came from and put myself back through the mill yet again, but can simply point and say where it hurts - and **I** am the one whose attention in the end, moves and restores these energy blockages, gives permission and the instruction for healing to be executed, it is all **my** choice, **my** doing.

When I come out of the session as a client, I AM PROUD OF WHAT I HAVE ACHIEVED. I am grateful, immensely grateful to the practitioner who assisted me, but it is my very own gain, my very own triumph.

Lastly, as I am doing this, the very fact that my various bizarre emotions, thoughts and behaviours are simply structural and systemic responses to a deeply disturbed and injured energy body beneath, and NOT signs of madness, that God doesn't love me or that I've deserved any of this is simply a cooling rain to a fire of pain which has smouldered for 40 years or more.

Those are my own responses to EmoTrance exercises when I take part in person.

Those types of responses are mirrored by the other participants and indeed, in this case so very powerfully so that I have to conclude it is not only me who finds this way of working with old problems incredibly relieving from both angles - that of the practitioner, and that of the therapist. I actually had *wanted* to hug some of the participants, and I don't touch nor hug unless the cavalry is standing by and I've basically given birth myself to the person in question! Others there said that their practice partners "came to life before their eyes", that they felt the others in the room "became so much more real" and some remarked that they had "never before felt so connected to a client" as they had done during these exercises.

THAT is perhaps the most truly amazing and profound effect of EmoTrance and where as far as I am concerned, the greatest hope for further healing and resolution resides for those amongst us who, like myself, have lost it somewhere with the human race, have crept off in pain and defeat to hide behind their shields just so they might survive another day without going completely insane and have remained there, disconnected, lonely and slowly "starving for love amidst the oceans of energy".

What I also did see and experience so profoundly that I think I've finally learned is that working with the energy body in this way and entirely honouring the PHYSIOLOGICAL responses of the body is perhaps the master key to a true re-connection of consciousness, energy body and physicality in the end.

I've had a very brief personal experience of what happens when that happens, when all of you comes into sync just for a flash of a moment - it is a sense of lucidity and presence, of connection and incredible clarity of mind which encompasses all that IS indeed just like an enlightenment state, an epiphany, a numinous experience. I had this brief experience during this training, and you could say that it has re-set my goal posts as to what it is that I'm trying to achieve, what I'm actually after, and what can be done if we get this right.

Silvia Hartmann, Creator, EmoTrance, 2003

If You Can Feel It, You Can Heal It!

A Magical Energy Transformation Experience

By Janet Dedman

My very first experience of EmoTrance was a one-day workshop with Sandra Hillawi – the first of a two-day Practitioner's Course. It was a brilliant summer's day, blue sky, fluffy white clouds and our small group were gathered at a beautiful country house near Bath in the United Kingdom.

But my heart was far from sunny. A black cloud of fear and sadness hung over me, as my relationship with my partner was under strain and I knew he wanted to split up and sell our home. This was a great worry to me, as when my ex-husband had remarried he'd stopped supporting my son, who was at drama school and, due to the stress I'd been under, my business wasn't doing very well either. I was really scared that, on my own, I'd never be able to afford to get a new home for the two of us and support my son through the rest of his course.

I knew deep down that my fear and negativity were very counter-productive and that I should try to overcome them, but however hard I tried nothing was working. So when we started practising EmoTrance on one another, I plucked up the courage to confide in my partner and work on the problem with her.

As we sat on a wooden bench in the shade of a small tree, she gently encouraged me to connect with my feelings of fear and insecurity. I took some deep breaths and concentrated on the process of releasing. I was amazed at how quickly I felt calmer and how soon I found myself much more relaxed about the situation, even though in reality, my circumstances had not changed. It was almost unbelievable and I wondered whether it would hold.

I need not have worried. The very next day I received a letter from my partner's solicitor confirming my worst fears. I opened it while we were having breakfast together and casually tossed it onto the table with the calm remark "Oh, so that's why you've been acting so strangely lately." My reaction shocked me – but nothing like how much it shocked my partner!

Over the following years I have continued to use EmoTrance on myself and it has pulled me through every challenge I encountered – my break-up, house move, supporting my son through his course, making a new home for us and re-building my business in another town.

I have also had the joy of sharing its gentle power with my clients and helping them overcome fears and phobias, break through depression, transform poor relationships, enhance self-esteem and beat emotional eating disorders.

Earlier this year I also trained as an EmoTrance trainer.

I believe that, with EmoTrance, whatever your problem, if you can feel it, you can heal it.

Janet Dedman, 2007
EmoTrance Practitioner & Trainer
Gloucestershire, United Kingdom
01453 542272
janet_dedman@hotmail.com

EmoTrance Short Reviews

Since its first presentation in 2002, EmoTrance has gathered rave reviews from thousands of delighted practitioners and all kinds of people who have found relief, release and joy of life in "The Oceans Of Energy".

Here are a few short reviews from many people, from many countries and backgrounds, from all around the World.

EmoTrance Reviews In Brief

"Of all the many therapies I've trained in and approaches I have used none have excited me and touched me so deeply. EmoTrance is quite simply the most beautiful, graceful and simple healing and self-care approach I have come across." - Dr Mark Atkinson

"The whole concept of EmoTrance is so very exciting … an empowering experience." - Sri Diamond

"Of course I was very sceptical about EmoTrance but my experience has shown me how effective and intoxicating it can be to pay attention to the energies in the body and to let them find their way out." - Gottfried Sumser

"EmoTrance is a quantum leap forward to the truth and something that has been there all the time just waiting to be re-discovered." - Gill Oliver

"In this day in time, when I see so many listless people, whose lives are at best mundane, and realistically are virtually joyless, the prospect of assisting them to find joy is thrilling to me." - Linda Economides

"EmoTrance is such a beautiful way to help heal our world effectively and efficiently, ultimately on a large scale." - Jennine Allen

"EmoTrance is amazingly simple and yet very effective and powerful." - Corinne Alexandre

"I came with an open mind and was extremely impressed. Very beneficial and powerful. EmoTrance is a useful tool that I can use alongside my other skills." - Linda Spencer

"I feel amazed at both the simplicity and the power of EmoTrance." - Ela Burton

"EmoTrance gets down to the crux of emotional and physical issues without any jargon or superficial overlay." - Pat Wynne

"EmoTrance is a fantastic healing tool to be used on its own or in conjunction with other therapies." - Nigel Deans

"After exploring numerous energy healing modalities, EmoTrance is the only one with which I have finally made significant shifts in my spiritual, emotional, mental, and physical condition: from heaviness to lightness; from depression to joy, from fatigue to high energy." - Robert Smith

"The feedback and results from my clients have been amazing, and I feel much more empowered while attending to any situation of my own personal and business life."- Figen Genco

"I consider EmoTrance to be the most important spiritual breakthrough this millennium so far." - Eolake Stubblehouse

"I believe that my patients will really appreciate the deep elegance of EmoTrance." - Baya Salmon-Hawk

"EmoTrance is an amazing experience of just how good you can feel, how much more powerful you can be and how much more there is waiting - just for you." - Steve Bishop

"I have found is that EmoTrance is an easy, simple and refreshing way to do what we are here for, to grow and develop with each other." - Larry Hanus

"I began applying EmoTrance to every negative emotional feelings that I have, and boy does it work. In fact I have temporarily put EFT aside in favour of EmoTrance which is much easier and faster for emotional stuff." - Phua HH

"In EmoTrance, I have found the process that I have been waiting for my entire life. Finally I feel as though I can not only put my own past behind me, but to help others achieve spiritual freedom too. This is a gift of immeasurable proportions to me." - Anne Henning

"EmoTrance is a process that is simple, spiritual, non-invasive, yet powerful and empowering to both the client and the practitioner." - Jane Riddick

"To be able to assist someone within a very short time reclaim calm, joy and tranquillity without giving up their own sense of power, without medications, without feeling less than, is a gift to be shared." - Mitzi Cline

"I find EmoTrance not only to not conflict with other methods, it is like that last piece of a jig saw puzzle that clicks everything into place." - Donald Mitchell

"I want to sing and dance and shout to the world, "Hey everybody, hear this. Come and truly enjoy life. Come alive. Look, what a magical world we are living in. We are in paradise Now. There is no need to suffer anymore! There is no need!" - Mohammed Abdul-Razak

"What I am really excited about are the possibilities Silvia Hartmann is outlining in this work. This is what I want, this is what every one of my clients wants." - Jim Hermann

"My personal experience with EmoTrance has been wonderfully rewarding." - Joan Hitlin

"I originally trained as a hypnotherapist and have practised both hypnotherapy and MET's for the past few years. I have been playing with EmoTrance recently and I love it." - Chrissie Hardisty

"I have had awesome results with EmoTrance and am using it every day with clients. One of the biggest rewards is the laughter at the end of a session when all becomes clear!" - Trisha Selmes

"I am thrilled with EmoTrance." - Maryanna Tracey

"I want to thank Silvia Hartmann for her wonderful discovery and excellent creation of the EmoTrance protocol to go with it." - Jeanette Pettiford

"I am completely in love with EmoTrance. The amazement and delight of realizing what is happening, and the possibilities dawning. Incredible watching all that light up people's eyes." - Debbie Phillips

"My wife LOVES EmoTrance. She took to it beautifully and has used this elegant technique to resolve some difficult situational issues." - Tres Schaffer

"It is thrilling to know that I am working with the Creative Order, helping people function in the way they are designed to." - Helena Svedin

"Fascinating, that it can be so easy and magnificent to help people out." - Manuela Csikor

"The possibilities for healing myself and others really does seem limitless. EmoTrance is so simple and yet so profound." - Bob Huffman

"What excites me most is that EmoTrance is simple and totally client centred." - Tony Birdfield

"With EmoTrance the best part is working on an emotion as it happens! Immediate healing!" - Dawn Bradley

"What attracts me to EmoTrance is the sheer ease of application sans the religious dogma or lineage prejudices typically associated with other forms of healing." - Charles Austin

"EmoTrance is so easy to learn and do, it is delightful. Since I have learned EmoTrance, I cannot tell you how much joy it has brought into my life." - Margarita Foley

"EmoTrance is such an easy process and so natural!" - Lutz Stradmann

"I felt physical sensations I hadn't experienced before, in places I had never experienced any sensations at all!" - Helen Ryle

"Silvia Hartmann has taken the revolutionary new field of energy therapy to the next level." - Lyman Griffin

"The EmoTrance process is simple to use and to learn. It can be applied almost anywhere. The principle allows one to connect to

almost all aspects of living, and of the nature around us." - John Mathai

"My mission is healing and EmoTrance is the instrument I was looking for to improve my healing work." - Eliza Spetter

"EmoTrance is not just a tool for healing and transformation, it has brought me to a new level of awareness and a new way of being." - Sandra Hillawi

"This EmoTrance process is dramatically decreasing the amount of reflexology treatments clients require because I can help them release emotions I can see are related to their condition. The two combined excellently together." - Kath Baker

"Dump Negative or Painful Memories - by learning a simple but effective technique called EmoTrance." - Alice Hart-Davis

"What I find most exciting about EmoTrance are the wonderful results I've already been able to achieve and am continuing to achieve using this modality. I also find it great that EmoTrance offers such a powerful, yet simple way of facilitating remarkable changes quickly and easily." - David Fleming

"EmoTrance creates deep, lasting change that you can feel." - Sophie Goldstein

"I am very drawn to the EmoTrance modality because it gives great potential for bringing about wellness, both for myself and for future clients, in a deep and lasting way." - Jyoti Phull

"I found EmoTrance very exciting, definitely an answer to my prayers of how I can help a person heal when their spirit is weak." - Christy L'Angel

"The most attractive and convincing fact about EmoTrance is that it is based on the Even Flow of the Creative Order. A thoroughful and sensitive assisting behaviour of the practitioner being on an equal level with the client." - Alfred Scheib

EmoTrance Short Reviews

"EmoTrance is easy and able to be accomplished by anyone, empowers people to realize they are not at the total mercy of someone else and do have some control over their own lives." - Diane Sprigg

"EmoTrance is truly the cutting edge of where & how I can experience and help facilitate healing at this moment in my evolution." - Dylan Newcomb

"EmoTrance is not only a stand alone but "the" great bolt-on therapy. Wonderful." - Tom Wynn

"EmoTrance is simple, portable and easy." - Adam Wilson

"The beauty of EmoTrance is that it helps the individual to get back in touch with their own feedback systems." - Robin DeStefani

"EmoTrance can literally do the world for your clients. It can make a world of difference to you in every way." - Sandra Hillawi

"What I am really excited about are the possibilities Silvia Hartmann is outlining in this work. This is what I want, this is what everyone of my clients wants." - Jim Hermann

"I have been studying human changework for two decades, and in my experience, there is simply nothing as elegant and effective as Silvia Hartmann's EmoTrance. It's a work of genius." - Troy DeChampes

"EmoTrance is not only safe but an absolute joy to work with, it lifts and brightens the spirit, that's part of its design, you cannot fail to feel better, a fabulous by product of this simple but profound method." - Nicola Quinn

"I always found the tapping energy therapies too mechanical for my liking. EmoTrance allows your own healing powers to come out, it creates transformative experiences for healer and client alike." - Steve Collins

"My partner and I are very grateful to have discovered EmoTrance and be able to use it during our daily life." - Linda Austin

EmoTrance Short Reviews

"EmoTrance has changed my life! I read Oceans of Energy a few months ago and it has had such a profound effect on my everyday life, I love it! I only wish I'd found it earlier." - Kelly Mayne

"EmoTrance is such a beautiful way to help heal our world effectively and efficiently, ultimately on a large scale." - Jennine Allen

"Learning EmoTrance has been such a fabulous thing for me. I recommend it highly!" - Gaura Chandra

"EmoTrance is the missing step between logic and emotions." — Alex Kent

"I move around very freely these days, in a way that I hadn't been able to for a long time before I tried EmoTrance - and I feel great." - Bob Collier

"What I love about EmoTrance is that it helps us to relearn to use the systems we have been given to naturally process all the energies we encounter." - Susan Courtney

"EmoTrance is adding new dimensions that have sent my head spinning. I can barely imagine what we will be doing with this technique in 6 months, what to speak of 6 years time." - Ananga Sivyer

"Gets down to the crux of emotional and physical issues without any jargon or superficial overlay" - Pat Wynne

"A fantastic healing tool to be used on its own or in conjunction with other therapies." - Nigel Deans

"I'm a Thought Field Therapy trainer and know the effects of energy therapies, but this is a true diamond as the star is in the night sky! EmoTrance is the crest jewel in the crown of energy therapies. I love it!" - Tyicia Silvyell

"After having passed nearly every school of Meridian Therapies and Energy psychology I think that EmoTrance seems to be the one method that is nearest to the origin of were all the achievements of the other techniques come from." - Verena Stollnberger

"EmoTrance is fast, natural, elegant – and extremely powerful." - James Masterson

"What I find most exciting about EmoTrance is its simplicity and straight-forward approach to energy healing. It is direct, and, what is even better, it works." - Wellington Rodrigues

"I never experienced another way of treating psychological problems in such a brilliant, effective yet logical and natural way. EmoTrance is a huge step forward for every health professional and for mankind as a whole." - Gerald Stiehler

"Nothing in my considerable experience approaches the gentleness, joy and intelligence of EmoTrance." - Nan Rathjen

"EmoTrance can change your life forever and for the best. I know it did for me." - Tom de Kok

"I've trained in what seems like a thousands therapies – and get a lot out of all of them. However, my husband is a scientist so he really only gets on with EmoTrance. He says it's the only one that stands up under scrutiny, doesn't involve guesswork and is so logical that you really can't argue with it." - Katherine, US

"One light after the other went on in my head - of course! So simple, so powerful and so ****true*****! Brilliant, brilliant work and I am just overwhelmed with the sheer possibilities and potential of using this amazing system for – EVERYTHING!" - Shawna Lourette

"I absolutely loved the EmoTrance workshop, and am using it a LOT, for myself, and with my clients all over the world." - Susan, US

"What a wonderful, energising privilege and humbling experience to see and be a part of the transformations that took place. The changes were incredible, a fabulous experience for all of us." - Lisa Bundfuss

"Perhaps because the method bears similarities to the way I work with traumatised patients (I am a craniosacral therapist), EmoTrance really gels with me. So easy and yet so powerful." - Jon G Cassell

"EmoTrance can work wonders under very harsh circumstances, and work immediately." - J Allen

"It is only a short time that I have known EmoTrance and already wonderful things have happened!" - Detlev Tesch

"I have been working extensively with EmoTrance since the first training in 2002 with great success in many areas of emotional trauma. Since those 3 days in Kensington I have been on the most wonderful journey of discovery." - John C. Bunker

"It has been a fantastic year for me - EmoTrance has enabled me to go and enjoy myself - something that I have not done for a long time." - Leslie Ackerman

"Time and time again I am left speechless and amazed at the incredible results I am achieving with this gloriously simple, loving system that is EmoTrance." - Jutta Kirchner

"I can't begin to tell you how my life has changed and how many doors have opened for thanks to EmoTrance. It's a living miracle!" - Jeremy Baker

"EmoTrance manages to illustrate without pretentiousness the quintessence of energy psychology." - Haus Casser

"Over the years following my original training I have continued to use EmoTrance on myself and it has pulled me through every challenge I encountered." - Janet Dedman

"EmoTrance is so incredibly simple and magically powerful. It is as simple as lighting up a match and watching all the darkness disappear, no matter how old and ancient the darkness is." - Mohammed Abdul-Razak

EmoTrance.

REAL Energy Magic For The 3rd Millennium.

Your Path To EmoTrance

How To Learn EmoTrance – Step by Step

EmoTrance is a very interesting modality in so far that at the top level, it is really simple to learn and to do, but the more you know about it, the more profoundly fascinating it becomes and the more you can do with it.

Here is the suggested EmoTrance learning progression.

Becoming Interested In EmoTrance

First, read the EmoTrance Yearbook which will give you a good overview over the basic techniques, case examples for using EmoTrance in the real world, some self help sample techniques to try and many different EmoTrance articles to demonstrate what this can do for people just like you.

You can also visit www.EmoTrance.com to read more articles and get the latest news from the field, and there is a free EmoTrance chat group which is open to all at:

http://www.yahoogroups.com/group/EmoTrance2/

If you like what you have gathered so far, and you decide you would like to know more, the next step is ...

The Original EmoTrance Manual "Oceans Of Energy"

To study this book is by far a more efficient way of learning about EmoTrance properly; "Oceans Of Energy" by Silvia Hartmann explains clearly what EmoTrance is, what it does beyond mere healing and system alleviation, and is suitable for both existing healing practitioners as well as individual persons interested in using the techniques and approaches to supercharge their personal development plans.

Oceans of Energy contains all the groundbreaking Level 1 EmoTrance techniques and exercises, as well as many additional resources including case stories and the developmental history of EmoTrance.

An easy and cost effective way to bring what you have learned in the manual to life is to ...

A Personal Experience With A Licensed EmoTrance Practitioner

Although EmoTrance is an excellent self help system, its real power is revealed when the session is guided by an experienced EmoTrance practitioner. This is particularly the case for deeply repressed and frightening materials or issues that have seemed immovable and as hard as rock. For this, book a personal or telephone appointment with a registered EmoTrance Practitioner in your country who speaks your language.

You will have the personal attention of a professional person who will do their best to teach you the basic process and answer your questions at a very reasonable cost. This also often unlocks the self help success of EmoTrance and moves it up to a whole new level.

Ask your local practitioner for a FREE 15 minute "Try EmoTrance For Free!" experience. Most practitioners will be more than happy to share the joy of EmoTrance with you.

Practice EmoTrance!

Once you know what the basic EmoTrance process feels like, you have experienced the transformational "energized end state" and you know how to set the EmoTrance processes into motion, it is best to work with this for a while, to get to know it better and find out many things about your own energy body in the process. Many people also try it out on others - their family and friends, and if they are healers or therapists, on their clients. The next step on from this is to attend an ...

Official EmoTrance Personal Development Workshop

Most trainers provide low cost, one day personal experience or personal development workshops. During such a workshop, not only do you get to work on your own issues, but you will also learn more of the finer points of the techniques and become aware of many more applications and circumstances in which EmoTrance can be most helpful. In working and discussing EmoTrance with others, you achieve a new depth of understanding and skill, and of course, you can also ask for personal help from the trainer and the assistants during the workshop.

Healers and therapists then have the option of going on to ...

The Official EmoTrance Practitioner Certification Training Workshop

In the practitioner training, the true depth of EmoTrance and its many patterns and techniques really becomes revealed. You will learn about shields, about your own healing powers, about repairing damage to the Energy Body and about the many different manifestations of energetic injuries, blockages and misalignments. The practitioner trainings also pick up on the underpinning theories of EmoTrance; but as with all EmoTrance training, they represent a particular opportunity to both experience ET healing and release as well as to be able to help facilitate it - a truly extraordinary experience which is the famous "Client-Practitioner Dance" at the heart of the EmoTrance System. From April 2006, EmoTrance Practitioners are licensed to conduct EmoTrance Healing Circles, and the relevant materials for this are a part of the official EmoTrance Practitioner Manual.

Visit the website for the latest up-to-date listings of trainings:

http://www.EmoTrance.com/

The EmoTrance DL Course

As an alternative or if there is no trainings scheduled in your country, there is the official Distance Learning EmoTrance Practitioner Certification course. This course allows you to study EmoTrance anywhere in the world in the comfort of your own home and it contains all the content and manuals of the live trainings PLUS unique and compensatory exercises, and comes with personal tutor support.

The EmoTrance Practitioner certification gives you everything you need as a professional healer, therapist or holistic health practitioner to be able to combine EmoTrance with your existing modalities, as well as offering EmoTrance sessions as a unique stand alone modality to help people with emotional problems.

For those who wish to go to the furthest cutting edge of EmoTrance's new energy technology, there is the ...

The Advanced EmoTrance Practitioner Certification Training

Since April 2006, certified EmoTrance Practitioners (ETPs) can take part in the Advanced Practitioner Workshop. This two day training is by no means more of the same, but covers the truly revolutionary and advanced energy techniques as outlined in Living Energy, The Patterns & Techniques of EmoTrance Vol. II, and Energy Magic, The Patterns & Techniques of EmoTrance Vol. III. Intense, amazing, deeply moving and exciting for the experienced practitioner, the advanced EmoTrance workshop presents a real opportunity to work directly with important aspects of the energy system, including the Higher Energetic Operating Systems HEROS.

The EmoTrance Trainer's Training

EmoTrance is a hugely successful and extremely popular healing modality - there is simply nothing like it in the world.

Amongst the real benefits of EmoTrance are:

- The immediate impact on the way we feel and think;
- The absence of religious dogma which makes EmoTrance completely acceptable to all major world religions without causing a conflict of faith;
- The sheer elegance and ease of use; the logic of the theory behind EmoTrance;
- The fact that no touching needs to take place to produce really profound healing experiences, making EmoTrance suitable for clinical settings and clients where touching is not allowed or impossible;
- The safety and comfort of the uncompromisingly client-led techniques;
- The way it empowers both client and practitioner equally;
- How EmoTrance dovetails so beautifully with literally any serious and correct healing approach, holistic, psychological or allopathic alike, without conflict or competition;
- That EmoTrance is so easy to learn for any human being and does not require ANY previous knowledge at all;

... and not least of all, that EmoTrance is so hopeful, pro-active, positive and joyful in essence.

All of these and the user friendly, simple techniques make EmoTrance an excellent choice for any existing health practitioner who has long wanted to include the benefits of energy healing into their practice, but felt that the existing approaches were simply too esoteric, too complicated, or too off putting to their clients, colleagues or supervisors.

As an officially certified EmoTrance Trainer, you can choose where and with whom you wish to work. EmoTrance is a fantastic benefit and add on to any kinesiologist, reflexologist, coaches, hypnotherapist, NLP-, Reiki-, Chi Gung-, Feng Shui practitioner, to mention but a few; but it is also the first choice for all those professionals working under supervision, including psychologists, doctors, social workers, teachers, priests, counsellors, and nurses.

EmoTrance is logical and immediately verifiable in personal experience. This means it can be used with groups and clients who would be very uncomfortable with or resistant to the older, more esoteric energy approaches, such as corporate clients, religious organisations, the military, and sports and performance clients, to name but a few.

EmoTrance Trainers can of course also conduct special interest workshops for the general public on any topic of their choice and including relationships, stress, addictions, weight loss, fitness, confidence and many, many more; introduction programmes of varying length; and the trainers are provided with fantastic back-up workshop manuals and support materials to make it as easy and delightful to teach an EmoTrance workshop, as it is to attend one.

For forthcoming EmoTrance Trainer's Trainings, please check the announcements on: www.EmoTrance.com

Here are the resources once more in brief:

- FREE Introduction Ebook "The EmoTrance Yearbook"
- The EmoTrance Discussion Group at:
  http://www.YahooGroups.com/group/EmoTrance2/
- The Official EmoTrance Techniques Manual Oceans Of Energy available from all good bookshops and from:
  http://www.DragonRising.com/

- Find A Licensed EmoTrance Practitioner in the Yearbook or at:
  http://www.EmoTrance.com/
- Find A Licensed live EmoTrance workshop at:
  http://www.EmoTrance.com/
- The Official EmoTrance Practitioner Certification Home Study Course at:
  http://www.EmoTrance.com/

Learn to truly master your emotions.

**Experience the world as it was designed to be –
Beautiful, Fascinating and Enriching.**

Transform your understanding of the world.

Transform your relationships.

Transform your expectations and your achievements.

Bring hope and delight to others.

Learn to live in joy and abundance – in the REAL world.

Welcome To The Wonderful World Of EmoTrance!

EmoTrance Members Directory

EmoTrance Trainers

Australia

John Bunker
Emotional Freedom Today
Richmond, New South Wales, Australia
www.EmoTrance.com/m/john_bunker
61419149576

Austria

Christiana Kriechbaum-Hinteregger
Vienna, Wien, Austria
EmoTrance.com/m/christiana_kriechbaum_hinteregger
http://www.holisticwell.com
(Austria) +43 676 45 44 042

Canada

Gisèle Bourgoin
Québec, Quebec, Canada
www.EmoTrance.com/m/gisle_bourgoin
http://giselebourgoin.alchymed.com

Chile

Paul Dawidowicz
Marnuevo SA
Providencia, Santiago, Chile
www.EmoTrance.com/m/paul_dawidowicz
http://www.marnuevo.com

Croatia

Christiana Kriechbaum-Hinteregger
Croatia
EmoTrance.com/m/christiana_kriechbaum_hin
teregger
http://www.holisticwell.com
(Austria) +43 676 45 44 042

England

Marie Andersen
Insight Personal and Professional Development Ltd
Yeovil, Somerset, England
www.EmoTrance.com/m/marie_andersen
01935 840 256

Danica Apolline
Enfield, England
www.EmoTrance.com/m/danica_apolline
http://www.thebigchi.com
07967 108 024

Kath Baker
Havant, Hampshire, England
www.EmoTrance.com/m/kath_baker
02392 365 318

Jayne Bartlett
Southampton, Hampshire, England
www.EmoTrance.com/m/jayne_bartlett
02380 739 839

Sonja Beacham
Nottingham, Nottinghamshire, England
www.EmoTrance.com/m/sonja_beacham
http://excellencewithin.com
0845 408 9378

Tony Birdfield
Poole, Dorset, England
www.EmoTrance.com/m/tony_birdfield
http://www.the-healing-space.net
01202 601 412

Louise Bliss
Emotional Freedom Training
Northolt, Middlesex, England
www.EmoTrance.com/m/louise_bliss
http://emotionalfreedom-training.co.uk
0208 845 1293 or 07811 447070

Kim Bradley
Emotional Freedom Training
Hayes, Middlesex, England
www.EmoTrance.com/m/kim_bradley
http://emotionalfreedom-training.co.uk
020 8842 2386 or 07970 584 851

Catherine Britcliffe
Equilibrium
Clitheroe, Lancashire, England
EmoTrance.com/m/catherine_britcliffe
http://catherinebritcliffe.co.uk
01200 444018

Lisa Bundfuss
Portishead, Somerset, England
www.EmoTrance.com/m/lisa_bundfuss
01275 844 855

Sally Canning
Worksop, Nottinghamshire, England
www.EmoTrance.com/m/sally_canning
http://innersolutions-uk.com
01909 472 097

Joanne Cox
Dorchester, Dorset, England
www.EmoTrance.com/m/joanne_cox
01300 341 331/0799

Chris Dawson
EmoTrance Trainer &
Advanced Practitioner
Stockport,Cheshire, UK
Tel: 0161 474 7996
www.stockport-hypnotherapy.co.uk

Janet Dedman, MCMA, MAMT,
EmoTrance Trainer,
Advanced Practitioner
& Holistic Therapist
OPTIMUM HEALTH &
PEACE OF MIND
the keys to your empowerment
Dursely, Glos, England, UK.
www.EmoTrance.com/m/janet_dedman
Tel: 01453 542 272

Rabea Dehghan
Ealing, London, England
www.EmoTrance.com/m/rabea_dehghan
0208 810 7346

Peter Delves
Kenilworth, Warwickshire, England
www.EmoTrance.com/m/peter_delves
http://delves.co.uk
01926 856 746

Margarita Foley
London, England
www.EmoTrance.com/m/margarita_foley
020 88019 883

Michele Gamble
London, England
www.EmoTrance.com/m/michele_gamble
07785971606

Debra Goldston
Clear Intentions
Moreton Nr. Newport, Shropshire, England
www.EmoTrance.com/m/debra_goldston
http://www.clear-intentions.co.uk
01952 691 542

Stacie Gray Debros
Uckfield, East Sussex, England
EmoTrance.com/m/stacie_gray_debros
01825 733 053

Ed Grimshaw
Generative Business Solutions
Clitheroe, England
www.EmoTrance.com/m/ed_grimshaw
+44 (0)1257 453 577

Mary Haines
Chichester, West Sussex, England
www.EmoTrance.com/m/mary_haines
http://relaxandperform.com

Sandra Hillawi
EmoTrance Master Trainer,
Advanced Practitioner and
author of "The Love Clinic"
Passion for Health Ltd, Gosport,
Hampshire, UK
+44 (0)2392 433 928
sandra@PassionForHealth.com
www.SandraHillawi.com

Jenny Johnstone
Warrington, Cheshire, England
www.EmoTrance.com/m/jenny_johnstone
http://www.changinu.com
01942 677 502

Philip Knox
Rudgwick, West Sussex, England
www.EmoTrance.com/m/philip_knox

Deborah Labuschagne
Hempton, Oxfordshire, England
EmoTrance.com/m/deborah_labuschagne
07834189579

Irene Lambert
Melbourne, Derbyshire, England
www.EmoTrance.com/m/irene_lambert
http://willowtherapy.co.uk
+44 (0)1332 863 290

Michelle Lourdes
Lightwater, Surrey, England
EmoTrance.com/m/michelle_lourdes
01276 472 322

Linda McCroft
Alternative Approach
Attleborough, Norfolk, England
www.EmoTrance.com/m/linda_mccroft
http://www.alternativeapproach.co.uk
01953 458092

EmoTrance Members Directory - Trainers

Suzanne Georgina Moody
Wellbeing Clinic
St Helier, Jersey, England
EmoTrance.com/m/suzanne_georgina_moody
01534 482136

Patricia Moreby
Insight Personal and Professional Development
Ltd
Chilthorne Domer, Somerset, England
www.EmoTrance.com/m/patricia_moreby
01789 841273

Ruth Morris
Freedom Of Life
Wickford, Essex, England
www.EmoTrance.com/m/ruth_morris
http://freedomoflife.com
01268 710 707

Karen Neil
Seaham, County Durham, England
www.EmoTrance.com/m/karen_neil
http://www.lifestyletherapies.org
0191 526 2095

Trevor Noble
Woodgreen, Nr Fordingbridge, Hampshire,
England
www.EmoTrance.com/m/trevor_noble
http://www.passiontobe.co.uk
01725 513 670

Maggie Noskeau
Need Counselling
Nottingham, Nottinghamshire, England
www.EmoTrance.com/m/maggie_noskeau
http://www.needcounselling.co.uk
0115 9735 807

Lilian Poultney
Rugby, Warwickshire, England
www.EmoTrance.com/m/lilian_poultney
http://www.lilianpoultney.co.uk
01788567033

Simon Purcell
London, England
www.EmoTrance.com/m/simon_purcell
07883 304 042

Nicola Quinn
Bexhill, East Sussex, England
www.EmoTrance.com/m/nicola_quinn
http://nicolaquinn.com
01424 733 478

Frank Quinton
Southampton, Hampshire, England
www.EmoTrance.com/m/frank_quinton
http://www.quillcomplementary.com
023 8048 2425

Nan Rathjen
Ashford, Kent, England
www.EmoTrance.com/m/nan_rathjen

Jo Russell Smith
Wiveliscombe, Somerset, England
EmoTrance.com/m/jo_russell_smith
http://www.A-Zestforlife.com
01984 623 642

Barbara Saph
EmoTrance Trainer &
Advanced Practitioner
Saphire Therapy, Hypnotherapy
& Energy Psychology
Marchwood, Southampton,
Hants SO40 4UN
02380663658
07919162542
SaphireEnergy@tiscali.co.uk
www.SaphireEnergyTherapies.co.uk

Sue Sawyer
Energy Benefits
Frith End, Nr. Borden, Hampshire, England
www.EmoTrance.com/m/sue_sawyer
http://www.energybenefits.com
0845 388 1128

Zena Shubbar
London, England
www.EmoTrance.com/m/zena_shubbar

Anne Sweet
East Molesey, Surrey, England
www.EmoTrance.com/m/anne_sweet
http://www.noninvasivetherapy.co.uk
02083982455

Karen Tinker
Karen Jane
Barnsley, Yorkshire, England
www.EmoTrance.com/m/karen_tinker
http://www.karenjane.co.uk
01226 380 681

France

Carol Borthwick
Caderousse 84860, Provence, France
www.EmoTrance.com/m/carol_borthwick
0033(0) 561 605 065

Mikael Cormont
Méru, France
www.EmoTrance.com/m/mikael_cormont
http://www.emotrance.fr

Germany

Regine Bialojan
Schmitten, Germany
www.EmoTrance.com/m/regine_bialojan
+49 6084 5445

Hartmut Gerber
Stuttgart, Germany
www.EmoTrance.com/m/hartmut_gerber
+49 (0)711 633 3209

Petra Groschupf
Merching, Germany
www.EmoTrance.com/m/petra_groschupf
http://petragroschupf.de
+498233-795980

Werner Jahn
Diesenhofen, Germany
www.EmoTrance.com/m/werner_jahn
89 6283 0330

Daniela Kuehn
Wesel, Germany
www.EmoTrance.com/m/daniela_kuehn
00492814607472

Antje Ottersdorf
Dummer Ot : Walsmuhlen, Mecklenburg, Germany
EmoTrance.com/m/antje_ottersdorf
http://www.herznoA.de
+49 3869 599456

Heike Schonert
einfach - frei LebensCoaching
Hagen, Germany
www.EmoTrance.com/m/heike_schonert
http://www.einfach-frei.de
+49 2334 41365 and +49 174 7779935

Gerald Stiehler
Muehltal, Germany
www.EmoTrance.com/m/gerald_stiehler
http://www.darmstadter-seminare.de
+49 (0)6151 520 9478

Detlev Tesch
Tesch Coaching & Training
Bonn, Germany
www.EmoTrance.com/m/detlev_tesch
http://emotrance.eu
+49 228 473792

Iran

Rabea Dehghan
No. 40 Sadaf Building, Tehran, Iran
www.EmoTrance.com/m/rabea_dehghan
0208 810 7346

Ireland

Ray Manning
Accomplish Change
Dublin 16, Ireland
www.EmoTrance.com/m/ray_manning
http://www.accomplishchange.com
00353-1- 298 6507

Israel

Varda Banilivy
Tel Aviv, Israel
www.EmoTrance.com/m/varda_banilivy
+1 516 353 8156

Northern Ireland

Heather Johnston
Belfast, Co Antrim, N. Ireland
EmoTrance.com/m/heather_johnston
028 90 709 488 or 028 90 792 365

The Netherlands

Mary Van Der Stam
Neuromind
Geldrop, Netherlands
EmoTrance.com/m/loretta_van_der_stam
http://neuromind.nl
+31 40 8428516

Margreet Vink
EmoTrance Nederland
Purmerend, Noordholland, Netherlands
www.EmoTrance.com/m/margreet_vink
http://emotrance.nl
0031-299-416444

Norway

Tom Soerevik
Bergen, Norway
www.EmoTrance.com/m/tom_soerevik
+ 4755 168 267

Scotland

Michele Gamble
Scotland
www.EmoTrance.com/m/michele_gamble
07785971606

Naomi Mandel
Aberdeen, Aberdeenshire, Scotland

www.EmoTrance.com/m/naomi_mandel
http://www.shamballa.org.uk
01224 321 110

Gordon Soutar
Edinburgh, Midlothian, Scotland
www.EmoTrance.com/m/gordon_soutar
http://www.complementary-therapy.com
0131 467 0238

Jo Spaczynska
Edinburgh, Midlothian, Scotland
www.EmoTrance.com/m/jo_spaczynska
http://www.a-zingtherapies.co.uk
0131 556 8878

Duncan Tennant
Livingston, West Lothian, Scotland
www.EmoTrance.com/m/duncan_tennant
01506 438153

Sweden

Ann-Sofi Forsberg
Provegeta
Löderup, Sweden
EmoTrance.com/m/ann_sofi_forsberg
http://www.centerforenergipsykologi.se
+46(0)411 527 030

Susann Forsberg
Bodyuniverse
Löderup, Sweden
www.EmoTrance.com/m/susann_forsberg
http://bodyuniverse.dk
+46-(0)709 733 947

Peter Lee
ring din Coach
Luleå, Sweden
www.EmoTrance.com/m/peter_lee
http://www.regnum.nu
0920-990 00

Sofia Olsson
Regnum
Luleå, Sweden
www.EmoTrance.com/m/sofia_olsson
http://www.regnum.nu
070-325 25 57

Switzerland

Danielle Meier
Ermensee, Luzern, Switzerland
www.EmoTrance.com/m/danielle_meier

Heidi Saputelli
Beinwil Am See, Aargau, Switzerland
www.EmoTrance.com/m/heidi_saputelli
062 772 02 34

Ursula Schweizer
Aarwangen, BE, Switzerland
EmoTrance.com/m/ursula_schweizer
http://www.vita-prax.ch
062 923 5557

Reto Wyss
Swiss Center for EFT
Herzogenbuchsee, Berne, Switzerland
www.EmoTrance.com/m/reto_wyss
http://www.coaching4success.ch
+41 62 962 9212

Beatrix Zeller
Berg-Dägerlen, Switzerland
www.EmoTrance.com/m/beatrix_zeller

Turkey

Inci Erkin
Alsancak, Izmir, Turkey
www.EmoTrance.com/m/inci_erkin
http://www.eftturkey.com
0090232 422 0365

United States

Francine Anderson
Tulsa, Oklahoma, United States
EmoTrance.com/m/francine_anderson

Vincent Bathea
Bathea Alternative Health Solutions
Dallas, Texas, United States
www.EmoTrance.com/m/vincent_bathea
http://www.batheaalternativehealthsolutions.com
+1 972 824 2079

Lorie Von S Brown
Freeport, New York, United States
EmoTrance.com/m/lorie_von_s_brown
917-445-6886

Abraham Bruck
Monsey, New York, United States
www.EmoTrance.com/m/abraham_bruck
http://thebruckgroup.com
718-687-8805

Mary Anne Cumbie
Cypress, Texas, United States
EmoTrance.com/m/mary_anne_cumbie

**Patricia DancingElk
EmoTrance Trainer &
Advanced Practitioner
Texas, United States
972-937-0377**
www.EmotranceTexas.com

Roberta Greene
Willingboro, New Jersey, United States
www.EmoTrance.com/m/roberta_greene
609-346-2132

Susan Grey
Columbia, South Carolina, United States
www.EmoTrance.com/m/susan_grey
http://www.distancehealer.net
803-419-3823

Janette Isaacson
Inner Radiance Inc
Redmond, Washington, United States
EmoTrance.com/m/janette_isaacson
206-755-6987

Rena Levin
Baltimore, Maryland, United States
www.EmoTrance.com/m/rena_levin
410-913-4057

Nan Rathjen
Lacey, Washington, United States
www.EmoTrance.com/m/nan_rathjen

Dottie Ward
Morton Grove, Illinois, United States
www.EmoTrance.com/m/dottie_ward
773/972 3789

Wales

Ruth Gilmore
Transformationsuk
Rhoose, Vale Of Glamorgan, Wales
www.EmoTrance.com/m/ruth_gilmore
01446 711464

Alicia Sawaya
Gwalchmai, Isle Of Anglesey, Wales
www.EmoTrance.com/m/alicia_sawaya
http://www. therapywales.co.uk
01407 720863

Suzi Tarrant
Narberth, Pembrokeshire, Wales
www.EmoTrance.com/m/suzi_tarrant
07941 261037

EmoTrance Advanced Practitioners

Australia

John Bunker
Richmond, New South Wales, Australia
www.EmoTrance.com/m/john_bunker
61419149576

Austria

Christiana Kriechbaum-Hinteregger
Vienna, Wien, Austria
EmoTrance.com/m/christiana_kriechbaum_hin
teregger
(Austria) +43 676 45 44 042

Canada

Gisèle Bourgoin
Québec, Quebec, Canada
www.EmoTrance.com/m/gisle_bourgoin

Chile

Paul Dawidowicz
Providencia, Santiago, Chile
www.EmoTrance.com/m/paul_dawidowicz

Croatia

Christiana Kriechbaum-Hinteregger
Croatia
EmoTrance.com/m/christiana_kriechbaum_hin
teregger
(Austria) +43 676 45 44 042

England

Sibel Akpolat
London, England
www.EmoTrance.com/m/sibel_akpolat
07775608561

Marie Andersen
Yeovil, Somerset, England
www.EmoTrance.com/m/marie_andersen
01935 840 256

Danica Apolline
Enfield, England
www.EmoTrance.com/m/danica_apolline
07967 108 024

Mark Atkinson
London, England
www.EmoTrance.com/m/mark_atkinson
08450946450

Kath Baker
Havant, Hampshire, England
www.EmoTrance.com/m/kath_baker
02392 365 318

Jayne Bartlett
Southampton, Hampshire, England
www.EmoTrance.com/m/jayne_bartlett
02380 739 839

Sonja Beacham
Nottingham, Nottinghamshire, England
www.EmoTrance.com/m/sonja_beacham
0845 408 9378

Louise Bliss
Northolt, Middlesex, England
www.EmoTrance.com/m/louise_bliss
0208 845 1293 or 07811 447070

Kim Bradley
Hayes, Middlesex, England
www.EmoTrance.com/m/kim_bradley
020 8842 2386 or 07970 584 851

Catherine Britcliffe
Clitheroe, Lancashire, England
EmoTrance.com/m/catherine_britcliffe
01200 444018

Lisa Bundfuss
Portishead, Somerset, England
www.EmoTrance.com/m/lisa_bundfuss
01275 844 855

Sally Canning
Worksop, Nottinghamshire, England
www.EmoTrance.com/m/sally_canning
01909 472 097

Joanne Cox
Dorchester, Dorset, England
www.EmoTrance.com/m/joanne_cox
01300 341 331/0799

Serap Danyildiz
London, England
www.EmoTrance.com/m/serap_danyildiz
07886 921894

Chris Dawson
EmoTrance Trainer &
Advanced Practitioner
Stockport,Cheshire, UK
Tel: 0161 474 7996
www.stockport-hypnotherapy.co.uk

Julie de Burgh
London, England
www.EmoTrance.com/m/julie_de_burgh
+44 (0)208 9977966

Janet Dedman, MCMA, MAMT,
EmoTrance Trainer,
Advanced Practitioner
& Holistic Therapist
OPTIMUM HEALTH &
PEACE OF MIND
the keys to your empowerment
Dursely, Glos, England, UK.
www.EmoTrance.com/m/janet_dedman
Tel: 01453 542 272

Rabea Dehghan
Ealing, London, England
www.EmoTrance.com/m/rabea_dehghan
0208 810 7346

Peter Delves
Kenilworth, Warwickshire, England
www.EmoTrance.com/m/peter_delves
01926 856 746

Christina Elvin
Northampton, Northamptonshire, England
www.EmoTrance.com/m/christina_elvin
01604 768 343

Margarita Foley
London, England
www.EmoTrance.com/m/margarita_foley
020 88019 883

Michele Gamble
London, England
www.EmoTrance.com/m/michele_gamble
07785971606

Debra Goldston
Moreton Nr. Newport, Shropshire, England
www.EmoTrance.com/m/debra_goldston
01952 691 542

Maria Grant
Blackburn, England
www.EmoTrance.com/m/maria_grant
01254 692245

Stacie Gray Debros
Uckfield, East Sussex, England
EmoTrance.com/m/stacie_gray_debros
01825 733 053

Ed Grimshaw
Clitheroe, England
www.EmoTrance.com/m/ed_grimshaw
+44 (0)1257 453 577

Mary Haines
Chichester, West Sussex, England
www.EmoTrance.com/m/mary_haines

Sandra Hillawi

EmoTrance Master Trainer,
Advanced Practitioner and
author of "The Love Clinic"
Passion for Health Ltd, Gosport,
Hampshire, UK
+44 (0)2392 433 928
sandra@PassionForHealth.com
www.SandraHillawi.com

Nicola Hok
London, England
www.EmoTrance.com/m/nicola_hok
0208 749 6952

Rosemary Homer
Bristol, England
www.EmoTrance.com/m/rosemary_homer
0117 9535724

Cheryl Hopkins
London, England
www.EmoTrance.com/m/cheryl_hopkins
0845 680 2729

Janet Johnson
Hornchurch, Essex, England
www.EmoTrance.com/m/janet_johnson
01708 444 519

Jenny Johnstone
Warrington, Cheshire, England
www.EmoTrance.com/m/jenny_johnstone
01942 677 502

Philip Knox
Rudgwick, West Sussex, England
www.EmoTrance.com/m/philip_knox

Deborah Labuschagne
Hempton, Oxfordshire, England
EmoTrance.com/m/deborah_labuschagne
07834189579

Irene Lambert
Melbourne, Derbyshire, England
www.EmoTrance.com/m/irene_lambert
+44 (0)1332 863 290

Michelle Lourdes
Lightwater, Surrey, England
EmoTrance.com/m/michelle_lourdes
01276 472 322

Linda McCroft
Attleborough, Norfolk, England
www.EmoTrance.com/m/linda_mccroft
01953 458092

Suzanne Georgina Moody
St Helier, Jersey, England
EmoTrance.com/m/suzanne_georgina_moody
01534 482136

Patricia Moreby
Chilthorne Domer, Somerset, England
www.EmoTrance.com/m/patricia_moreby
01789 841273

Ruth Morris
Wickford, Essex, England
www.EmoTrance.com/m/ruth_morris
01268 710 707

Nikhil Nair
Cambridge, Cambridgeshire, England
www.EmoTrance.com/m/nikhil_nair

Karen Neil
Seaham, County Durham, England
www.EmoTrance.com/m/karen_neil
0191 526 2095

Trevor Noble
Woodgreen, Nr Fordingbridge, Hampshire,
England
www.EmoTrance.com/m/trevor_noble
01725 513 670

Maggie Noskeau
Nottingham, Nottinghamshire, England
www.EmoTrance.com/m/maggie_noskeau
0115 9735 807

Tansie Ody
Higher Denham, Middlesex, England
www.EmoTrance.com/m/tansie_ody
07702 322699

Louise Player
Clevedon, North Somerset, England
www.EmoTrance.com/m/louise_player
01275 409809

Lilian Poultney
Rugby, Warwickshire, England
www.EmoTrance.com/m/lilian_poultney
01788567033

Simon Purcell
London, England
www.EmoTrance.com/m/simon_purcell
07883 304 042

Nicola Quinn
Bexhill, East Sussex, England
www.EmoTrance.com/m/nicola_quinn
01424 733 478

Frank Quinton
Southampton, Hampshire, England
www.EmoTrance.com/m/frank_quinton
023 8048 2425

Jo Russell Smith
Wiveliscombe, Somerset, England
EmoTrance.com/m/jo_russell_smith
01984 623 642

Beatrice Salmon-Hawk
Langford, Bedfordshire, England
EmoTrance.com/m/beatrice_salmon_hawk
01462 437350

Barbara Saph
EmoTrance Trainer &
Advanced Practitioner
Saphire Therapy, Hypnotherapy
& Energy Psychology
Marchwood, Southampton,
Hants SO40 4UN
02380663658
07919162542
SaphireEnergy@tiscali.co.uk
www.SaphireEnergyTherapies.co.uk

Sue Sawyer
Frith End, Nr. Borden, Hampshire, England
www.EmoTrance.com/m/sue_sawyer
0845 388 1128

Zena Shubbar
London, England
www.EmoTrance.com/m/zena_shubbar

Anne Sweet
East Molesey, Surrey, England
www.EmoTrance.com/m/anne_sweet
02083982455

Karen Tinker
Barnsley, Yorkshire, England
www.EmoTrance.com/m/karen_tinker
01226 380 681

France

Carol Borthwick
Caderousse 84860, Provence, France
www.EmoTrance.com/m/carol_borthwick
0033(0) 561 605 065

Mikael Cormont
Méru, France
www.EmoTrance.com/m/mikael_cormont

Germany

Gitta Berg
Furth-Brombach, Germany
www.EmoTrance.com/m/gitta_berg
+49 (0) 6253 3849, +49 (0) 172 6212984

Regine Bialojan
Schmitten, Germany
www.EmoTrance.com/m/regine_bialojan
+49 6084 5445

Petra Groschupf
Merching, Germany
www.EmoTrance.com/m/petra_groschupf
+498233-795980

Margit Heiter
Laupheim, Baden-Württemberg, Germany
www.EmoTrance.com/m/margit_heiter
07392/ 911847

Susanne Hoffmann
Braunschweig, Niedersachsen, Germany
EmoTrance.com/m/susanne_hoffmann
49 531 501913

Werner Jahn
Diesenhofen, Germany
www.EmoTrance.com/m/werner_jahn
89 6283 0330

Daniela Kuehn
Wesel, Germany
www.EmoTrance.com/m/daniela_kuehn
00492814607472

Renate Kustner
Igersheim, Baden-Württemberg, Germany
www.EmoTrance.com/m/renate_kustner
07931 - 44253

Antje Ottersdorf
Dummer Ot : Walsmuhlen, Mecklenburg,
Germany
EmoTrance.com/m/antje_ottersdorf
+49 3869 599456

Birgit Reinert
Stuttgart, Germany
www.EmoTrance.com/m/birgit_reinert
+49 711 632452

Elisabeth Rüttler
Baden Wurtemberg, Germany
EmoTrance.com/m/elisabeth_rttler
0793144765

Heike Schonert
Hagen, Germany
www.EmoTrance.com/m/heike_schonert
+49 2334 41365 and +49 174 7779935

Gerald Stiehler
Muehltal, Germany
www.EmoTrance.com/m/gerald_stiehler
+49 (0)6151 520 9478

Detlev Tesch
Bonn, Germany
www.EmoTrance.com/m/detlev_tesch
+49 228 473792

Birgit Ulrich-Reinisch
Leimen, Baden-Württemberg, Germany
EmoTrance.com/m/birgit_ulrich_reinisch1

Sabine Witzke
Maintal, Germany
www.EmoTrance.com/m/sabine_witzke
49 0 6109 62420

Iran

Rabea Dehghan
No. 40 Sadaf Building, Tehran, Iran
www.EmoTrance.com/m/rabea_dehghan
0208 810 7346

Ireland

Anna Casey
Dun Laoghaire, Co Dublin, Ireland
www.EmoTrance.com/m/anna_casey
(01) 284 3849

Cliona Farrell
Blackrock,, County Dublin, Ireland
www.EmoTrance.com/m/cliona_farrell
00353 (0)1 2881431

Ray Manning
Dublin 16, Ireland
www.EmoTrance.com/m/ray_manning
00353-1- 298 6507

Ita Mc Tigue
Drumcondra, Dublin, Ireland
www.EmoTrance.com/m/ita_mc_tigue
086 341 4788

Helen McCrarren
Scotstown, Co Monaghan, Ireland
www.EmoTrance.com/m/helen_mccrarren
00353 87412 9385

Nuala O'Rourke
Goatstown, Dublin, Ireland
www.EmoTrance.com/m/nuala_orourke
00 353 12982 642

Helen Ryle
Tralee, Co Kerry, Ireland
www.EmoTrance.com/m/helen_ryle
00353 87 773 4914

Tom Wynn
Dublin, Dublin, Ireland
www.EmoTrance.com/m/tom_wynn
00353 (1) 868 9596

Israel

Varda Banilivy
Tel Aviv, Israel
www.EmoTrance.com/m/varda_banilivy
+1 516 353 8156

Northern Ireland

Heather Johnston
Belfast, Co Antrim, N. Ireland
EmoTrance.com/m/heather_johnston
028 90 709 488 or 028 90 792 365

The Netherlands

Franklin Sluijters
Ulvenhout, Netherlands
EmoTrance.com/m/franklin_sluijters
+31 76 56 51 468

Mary Van Der Stam
Geldrop, Netherlands
EmoTrance.com/m/loretta_van_der_stam
+31 40 8428516

Margreet Vink
Purmerend, Noordholland, Netherlands
www.EmoTrance.com/m/margreet_vink
0031-299-416444

Norway

Tom Soerevik
Bergen, Norway
www.EmoTrance.com/m/tom_soerevik
+ 4755 168 267

Scotland

Michele Gamble
Scotland
www.EmoTrance.com/m/michele_gamble
07785971606

Naomi Mandel
Aberdeen, Aberdeenshire, Scotland
www.EmoTrance.com/m/naomi_mandel
01224 321 110

Gordon Soutar
Edinburgh, Midlothian, Scotland
www.EmoTrance.com/m/gordon_soutar
0131 467 0238

Jo Spaczynska
Edinburgh, Midlothian, Scotland
www.EmoTrance.com/m/jo_spaczynska
0131 556 8878

Duncan Tennant
Livingston, West Lothian, Scotland
www.EmoTrance.com/m/duncan_tennant
01506 438153

Sweden

Ann-Sofi Forsberg
Löderup, Sweden
EmoTrance.com/m/ann_sofi_forsberg
+46(0)411 527 030

Susann Forsberg
Löderup, Sweden
www.EmoTrance.com/m/susann_forsberg
+46-(0)709 733 947

Peter Lee
Luleå, Sweden
www.EmoTrance.com/m/peter_lee
0920-990 00

Sofia Olsson
Luleå, Sweden
www.EmoTrance.com/m/sofia_olsson
070-325 25 57

Switzerland

Werner Baumann
Zurich, Zh, Switzerland
www.EmoTrance.com/m/werner_baumann
0041 44 242 77 74

Beatrix Ellenberger Zeller
Neftenbach, Zh, Switzerland
EmoTrance.com/m/beatrix_zeller_ellenberger
0041 52 301 13 47

Beatrice Hinder
Sankt Gallen, Switzerland
www.EmoTrance.com/m/beatrice_hinder
+41 78 803 33 26

Priska Landis
Pfaeffikon, Schwyz, Switzerland
www.EmoTrance.com/m/priska_landis
+41 79 2323 500

Danielle Meier
Ermensee, Luzern, Switzerland
www.EmoTrance.com/m/danielle_meier

Silvia Müller
Grafenried, Bern, Switzerland
www.EmoTrance.com/m/silvia_mller
0041 31 767 81 07

Heidi Saputelli
Beinwil Am See, Aargau, Switzerland
www.EmoTrance.com/m/heidi_saputelli
062 772 02 34

Ursula Schweizer
Aarwangen, BE, Switzerland
EmoTrance.com/m/ursula_schweizer
062 923 5557

Reto Wyss
Herzogenbuchsee, Berne, Switzerland
www.EmoTrance.com/m/reto_wyss
+41 62 962 9212

Beatrix Zeller
Berg-Dägerlen, Switzerland
www.EmoTrance.com/m/beatrix_zeller

Martha Zryd
Norn, Tg, Switzerland
www.EmoTrance.com/m/martha_zryd
071 845 1560

Turkey

Inci Erkin
Alsancak, Izmir, Turkey
www.EmoTrance.com/m/inci_erkin
0090232 422 0365

United States

Francine Anderson
Tulsa, Oklahoma, United States
EmoTrance.com/m/francine_anderson

Vincent Bathea
Dallas, Texas, United States
www.EmoTrance.com/m/vincent_bathea
+1 972 824 2079

Lorie Von S Brown
Freeport, New York, United States
EmoTrance.com/m/lorie_von_s_brown
917-445-6886

Abraham Bruck
Monsey, New York, United States
www.EmoTrance.com/m/abraham_bruck
718-687-8805

Mary Anne Cumbie
Cypress, Texas, United States
EmoTrance.com/m/mary_anne_cumbie

Patricia DancingElk
EmoTrance Trainer &
Advanced Practitioner
Texas, United States
972-937-0377
www.EmotranceTexas.com

Roberta Greene
Willingboro, New Jersey, United States
www.EmoTrance.com/m/roberta_greene
609-346-2132

Susan Grey
Columbia, South Carolina, United States
www.EmoTrance.com/m/susan_grey
803-419-3823

Janette Isaacson
Redmond, Washington, United States
EmoTrance.com/m/janette_isaacson
206-755-6987

Rena Levin
Baltimore, Maryland, United States
www.EmoTrance.com/m/rena_levin
410-913-4057

Dottie Ward
Morton Grove, Illinois, United States
www.EmoTrance.com/m/dottie_ward
773/972 3789

Wales

Ruth Gilmore
Rhoose, Vale Of Glamorgan, Wales
www.EmoTrance.com/m/ruth_gilmore
01446 711464

Alicia Sawaya
Gwalchmai, Isle Of Anglesey, Wales
www.EmoTrance.com/m/alicia_sawaya
01407 720863

Suzi Tarrant
Narberth, Pembrokeshire, Wales
www.EmoTrance.com/m/suzi_tarrant
07941 261037

Lynne Theophanides
Cardiff, Wales
EmoTrance.com/m/lynne_theophanides
02920 259 520

EmoTrance Practitioners

Australia

John Bunker
Richmond, New South Wales, Australia
www.EmoTrance.com/m/john_bunker
61419149576

Wayne John Weavell
Australia
www.EmoTrance.com/m/wayne_weavell
61 438 356207

Austria

Christiana Kriechbaum-Hinteregger
Vienna, Wien, Austria
EmoTrance.com/m/christiana_kriechbaum_hin
teregger
(Austria) +43 676 45 44 042

Canada

Gisèle Bourgoin
Québec, Quebec, Canada
www.EmoTrance.com/m/gisle_bourgoin

Chile

Paul Dawidowicz
Providencia, Santiago, Chile
www.EmoTrance.com/m/paul_dawidowicz

Croatia

Christiana Kriechbaum-Hinteregger
Croatia
EmoTrance.com/m/christiana_kriechbaum_hinteregger
(Austria) +43 676 45 44 042

Denmark

Ann-Marie Nilsson
Copenhagen, Denmark
EmoTrance.com/m/ann_marie_nilsson
+46414440 240

Egypt

Zeinab Abdel Aziz Alloub
Cairo, Egypt
www.EmoTrance.com/m/zeinab_alloub
+20(0) 10 377 1616

Sahar Fouad Abdel Hay
Cairo, Egypt
EmoTrance.com/m/sahar_fouad_abdel_hay
+20(0) 10 141 9895

Khaled Al-Damalawy
Cairo, Egypt
EmoTrance.com/m/khaled_al_damalawy
+20(0)12 219 6392

Mervette Alloub
Cairo, Egypt
www.EmoTrance.com/m/
+20(0) 10 148 7755

Dalia El Gebaly
Cairo, Egypt
www.EmoTrance.com/m/dalia_el_gebaly
+20(0)10 657 3365

Neveen El-Gamal
Cairo, Egypt
www.EmoTrance.com/m/neveen_el_gamal
0020 105700601

Khaled El-Sharkawy
Cairo, Egypt
EmoTrance.com/m/khaled_el_sharkawy
+20(0)10 112 8057

Ezzat Ez Aldien
Cairo, Egypt
www.EmoTrance.com/m/ezzat_ez_aldien
+20(0) 12 312 1160

Dina Ghrasia Nouayem
Cairo, Egypt
EmoTrance.com/m/dina_ghrasia_nouayem
0020 22735 2594

England - Bedfordshire

Karen Haynes
Luton, Bedfordshire, England
www.EmoTrance.com/m/karen_haynes
01582 507594

Beatrice Salmon-Hawk
Langford, Bedfordshire, England
EmoTrance.com/m/beatrice_salmon_hawk
01462 437350

England - Berkshire

Sandra Hayes
Maidenhead, Berkshire, England
www.EmoTrance.com/m/sandra_hayes
01628 783 294

England - Bristol

Rosemary Homer
Bristol, England
www.EmoTrance.com/m/rosemary_homer
0117 9535724

Peter Nicholls
Bristol, England
www.EmoTrance.com/m/peter_nicholls
0117 3789943

Liz Vincent
Bristol, England
www.EmoTrance.com/m/liz_vincent
08454 300 183

England - Buckinghamshire

Inger Lise Howarth
Higher Denham, Buckinghamshire, England
EmoTrance.com/m/inger_lise_howarth
01895833779

England - Cambridgeshire

Nikhil Nair
Cambridge, Cambridgeshire, England
www.EmoTrance.com/m/nikhil_nair

England - Cheshire

Clare Ashley
Lymm, Cheshire, England
www.EmoTrance.com/m/clare_ashley
01925 755664

Chris Dawson
EmoTrance Trainer &
Advanced Practitioner
Stockport,Cheshire, UK
Tel: 0161 474 7996
www.stockport-hypnotherapy.co.uk

Jenny Johnstone
Warrington, Cheshire, England
www.EmoTrance.com/m/jenny_johnstone
01942 677 502

Pam Phelan
Wilmslow, Cheshire, England
www.EmoTrance.com/m/pam_phelan
01625 523426

Anne Stewart
Warrington, Cheshire, England
www.EmoTrance.com/m/anne_stewart
01925 450876

England – County Durham

Karen Neil
Seaham, County Durham, England
www.EmoTrance.com/m/karen_neil
0191 526 2095

England - Derbyshire

Maggie Hall
South Normanton, Derbyshire, England
www.EmoTrance.com/m/maggie_hall
01773580769

Irene Lambert
Melbourne, Derbyshire, England
www.EmoTrance.com/m/irene_lambert
+44 (0)1332 863 290

Clive Lawrence
Derby, Derbyshire, England
www.EmoTrance.com/m/clive_lawrence
01332 722 065

Pauline Oldrini
Belper, Derbyshire, England
www.EmoTrance.com/m/pauline_oldrini
01332 882677

Sereena Saroi
Derby, Derbyshire, England
www.EmoTrance.com/m/sereena_saroi

England - Dorset

Joanne Cox
Dorchester, Dorset, England
www.EmoTrance.com/m/joanne_cox
01300 341 331/0799

Ron Rosenfeld
Bournemouth, Dorset, England
www.EmoTrance.com/m/ron_rosenfeld
07807 657 413

England - Durham

Joanne Hewitt
Durham, England
www.EmoTrance.com/m/joanne_hewitt
0191 3789398

Robert Neil
Seaham, Durham, England
www.EmoTrance.com/m/robert_neil
07768828613

England – East Sussex

Clare Davison
Horsham, East Sussex, England
www.EmoTrance.com/m/clare_davison
01403 734 930

Stacie Gray Debros
Uckfield, East Sussex, England
EmoTrance.com/m/stacie_gray_debros
01825 733 053

Paul Lowe
Lewes, East Sussex, England
www.EmoTrance.com/m/paul_lowe
0870 879 8879

Nicola Quinn
Bexhill, East Sussex, England
www.EmoTrance.com/m/nicola_quinn
01424 733 478

Michael Schaefer
Burgess Hill, East Sussex, England
EmoTrance.com/m/michael_schaefer
+44 (0)1444 471147

Paul Sheppard
Hove, East Sussex, England
www.EmoTrance.com/m/paul_sheppard
07921819071

Isabel Zaplana
Burgess Hill, East Sussex, England
www.EmoTrance.com/m/isabel_zaplana
01444 471147

England - Essex

Tanya Dransfield
Leigh-On-Sea, Essex, England
EmoTrance.com/m/tanya_dransfield
01702 716168

Janet Johnson
Hornchurch, Essex, England
www.EmoTrance.com/m/janet_johnson
01708 444 519

Robert Kent
Essex, England
www.EmoTrance.com/m/robert_kent

Ruth Morris
Wickford, Essex, England
www.EmoTrance.com/m/ruth_morris
01268 710 707

Alexandra Raicar
Billericay, Essex, England
EmoTrance.com/m/alexandra_raicar
01277 654351

England - Gloucestershire

```
Janet Dedman, MCMA, MAMT,
EmoTrance Trainer,
Advanced Practitioner
& Holistic Therapist
OPTIMUM HEALTH &
PEACE OF MIND
the keys to your empowerment
Dursely, Glos, England, UK.
www.EmoTrance.com/m/janet_dedman
Tel: 01453 542 272
```

England – Greater Manchester

Pamela Ballard
Wigan, Greater Manchester, England
www.EmoTrance.com/m/pamela_ballard
01942 239 735

England - Hampshire

Kath Baker
Havant, Hampshire, England
www.EmoTrance.com/m/kath_baker
02392 365 318

Jayne Bartlett
Southampton, Hampshire, England
www.EmoTrance.com/m/jayne_bartlett
02380 739 839

Cassandra Burton
Basingstoke, Hampshire, England
EmoTrance.com/m/cassandra_burton
01256 476 837

Patricia Glasspool
Eastleigh, Hampshire, England
EmoTrance.com/m/patricia_glasspool
023 80 255 678

Jeanine Hanneman
Emsworth, Hampshire, England
EmoTrance.com/m/jeanine_hanneman
01243 373 460

Fiona Hickman Taylor
Portsmouth, Hampshire, England
EmoTrance.com/m/fiona_hickman_taylor
02392 359 676

```
Sandra Hillawi
EmoTrance Master Trainer,
Advanced Practitioner and
author of "The Love Clinic"
Passion for Health Ltd, Gosport,
Hampshire, UK
+44 (0)2392 433 928
sandra@PassionForHealth.com
www.SandraHillawi.com
```

Rosalind Horswell
Gosport, Hampshire, England
EmoTrance.com/m/rosalind_horswell
02392 355 455

Jen McFarlane
Marchwood, Southampton, England
www.EmoTrance.com/m/jen_mcfarlane

Trevor Noble
Woodgreen, Nr Fordingbridge, Hampshire, England
www.EmoTrance.com/m/trevor_noble
01725 513 670

Frank Quinton
Southampton, Hampshire, England
www.EmoTrance.com/m/frank_quinton
023 8048 2425

```
Barbara Saph
EmoTrance Trainer &
Advanced Practitioner
Saphire Therapy,  Hypnotherapy
& Energy Psychology
Marchwood, Southampton,
Hants SO40 4UN
02380663658
07919162542
SaphireEnergy@tiscali.co.uk
www.SaphireEnergyTherapies.co.uk
```

Sue Sawyer
Frith End, Nr. Borden, Hampshire, England
www.EmoTrance.com/m/sue_sawyer
0845 388 1128

Alison Linnell
Romsey, Hants, England
www.EmoTrance.com/m/alison_linnell

England - Hertfordshire

Marion Adams
St Albans, Hertfordshire, England
www.EmoTrance.com/m/marion_adams
07532 275339

Joy Salem
Radlett, Hertfordshire, England
www.EmoTrance.com/m/joy_salem
01923 854 154

England - Jersey

Suzanne Georgina Moody
St Helier, Jersey, England
EmoTrance.com/m/suzanne_georgina_moody
01534 482136

England - Kent

Bobbie Carcary
West Malling, Kent, England
www.EmoTrance.com/m/bobbie_carcary
01732 842990

Rachel Gay
Chiselhurst, Kent, England
www.EmoTrance.com/m/rachel_gay
0208 295 5955

Jenny Lye
Brook- Nr Ashford, Kent, England
www.EmoTrance.com/m/jenny_lye
01233 812 058

Rowana Rowan
Edenbridge, Kent, England
www.EmoTrance.com/m/rowana_rowan
01732 863 489

Angela Western
Tonbridge, Kent, England
www.EmoTrance.com/m/angela_western
01732 835 477

England - Lancashire

Catherine Britcliffe
Clitheroe, Lancashire, England
EmoTrance.com/m/catherine_britcliffe
01200 444018

Elaine Downs
Rossendale, Lancashire, England
www.EmoTrance.com/m/elaine_downs
01706 210257

Maria Grant
Blackburn, England
www.EmoTrance.com/m/maria_grant
01254 692245

Ed Grimshaw
Clitheroe, England
www.EmoTrance.com/m/ed_grimshaw
+44 (0)1257 453 577

Barbara Zell
Lytham St. Annes, Lancashire, England
www.EmoTrance.com/m/barbara_zell
01253 737 000

England - London

Mohammed Abdul-Razak
Leytonstone, London, England
EmoTrance.com/m/mohammed_abdul_razak
0208 558 5089

Sibel Akpolat
London, England
www.EmoTrance.com/m/sibel_akpolat
07775608561

Mark Atkinson
London, England
www.EmoTrance.com/m/mark_atkinson
08450946450

Andrea Barkhouche
London, England
EmoTrance.com/m/andrea_barkhouche
0208 340 4906

Alan Bridges
London, England
www.EmoTrance.com/m/alan_bridges
0207 71930056

Barry Cooper
London, England
www.EmoTrance.com/m/barry_cooper
020 8201 9967

Serap Danyildiz
London, England
www.EmoTrance.com/m/serap_danyildiz
07886 921894

Julie de Burgh
London, England
www.EmoTrance.com/m/julie_de_burgh
+44 (0)208 9977966

Rabea Dehghan
Ealing, London, England
www.EmoTrance.com/m/rabea_dehghan
0208 810 7346

Carol Edwards
London, England
www.EmoTrance.com/m/carol_edwards
0207 0130987

Chantal Fabrice
Eltham, London, England
www.EmoTrance.com/m/chantal_fabrice

Margarita Foley
London, England
www.EmoTrance.com/m/margarita_foley
020 88019 883

Michele Gamble
London, England
www.EmoTrance.com/m/michele_gamble
07785971606

Marie Hart
London, England
www.EmoTrance.com/m/marie_hart
0208 9062141

Nicola Hok
London, England
www.EmoTrance.com/m/nicola_hok
0208 749 6952

Cheryl Hopkins
London, England
www.EmoTrance.com/m/cheryl_hopkins
0845 680 2729

Jamie Passmore
London, England
www.EmoTrance.com/m/jamie_passmore
07859060486

Victoria Patrizia Pintus
London, England
EmoTrance.com/m/victoria_patrizia_pintus
0208 7894301

Simon Purcell
London, England
www.EmoTrance.com/m/simon_purcell
07883 304 042

Effie Rahs
Winchmore Hill, London, England
www.EmoTrance.com/m/effie_rahs
020 8245 0958

Helen Ryan
London, England
www.EmoTrance.com/m/helen_ryan
0208 9976254

Barbara Schurer
London, England
www.EmoTrance.com/m/barbara_schurer
0207 373 1452

Zena Shubbar
London, England
www.EmoTrance.com/m/zena_shubbar

Sally Topham
London, England
www.EmoTrance.com/m/sally_topham
020 7604 3619

Aneta Trojniak
London, England
www.EmoTrance.com/m/aneta_trojniak
04960845658

England - Middlesex

Danica Apolline
Enfield, England
www.EmoTrance.com/m/danica_apolline
07967 108 024

Louise Bliss
Northolt, Middlesex, England
www.EmoTrance.com/m/louise_bliss
0208 845 1293 or 07811 447070

Kim Bradley
Hayes, Middlesex, England
www.EmoTrance.com/m/kim_bradley
020 8842 2386 or 07970 584 851

Simon Caira
Ickenham, Middlesex, England
www.EmoTrance.com/m/simon_caira
07946474835

Karen Chagouri
Northolt, Middlesex, England
www.EmoTrance.com/m/karen_chagouri
07736809264

Geraldine Daly
Yeading, Middlesex, England
www.EmoTrance.com/m/geraldine_daly
07533 662708

Sandra Dickson
Greenford, Middlesex, England
www.EmoTrance.com/m/sandra_dickson
02085 759 835

Tansie Ody
Higher Denham, Middlesex, England
www.EmoTrance.com/m/tansie_ody
07702 322699

Liz Thurley
Shepperton, Middlesex, England
www.EmoTrance.com/m/liz_hurley
01932 269029

England – Newcastle-Upon-Tyne

Denise Jacques
Newcastle-Upon-Tyne, England
www.EmoTrance.com/m/denise_jacques
01207 271040

England - Norfolk

Tricia Davies
Norwich, Norfolk, England
www.EmoTrance.com/m/tricia_davies
01508 494441

Joanne Frost
Norwich, Norfolk, England
www.EmoTrance.com/m/joanne_frost
01603789387

Heather Johnson
Norwich, Norfolk, England
www.EmoTrance.com/m/heather_johnson

Linda McCroft
Attleborough, Norfolk, England
www.EmoTrance.com/m/linda_mccroft
01953 458092

Paula Stone
Carlton Rode, Norfolk, England
www.EmoTrance.com/m/paula_stone
01953 788722

England – North Devon

Liz Gilmour
Barnstaple, North Devon, England
www.EmoTrance.com/m/liz_gilmour
01271 861 141

Louise Player
Clevedon, North Somerset, England
www.EmoTrance.com/m/louise_player
01275 409809

England – North Yorkshire

Sandra Thompson
Cleveland, England
www.EmoTrance.com/m/sandra_thompson
01642 88104

England - Northamptonshire

Serena Chancellor
Northampton, Northamptonshire, England
EmoTrance.com/m/serena_chancellor
01604 843041

Christina Elvin
Northampton, Northamptonshire, England
www.EmoTrance.com/m/christina_elvin
01604 768 343

Mary Grace
Higham Ferrers, Northamptonshire, England
www.EmoTrance.com/m/mary_grace
01933 461 899

England - Nottinghamshire

Sonja Beacham
Nottingham, Nottinghamshire, England
www.EmoTrance.com/m/sonja_beacham
0845 408 9378

Shirley Broadhurst
Worksop, Nottinghamshire, England
EmoTrance.com/m/shirley_broadhurst
07840936535

Ela Burton
Nottingham, Nottinghamshire, England
www.EmoTrance.com/m/ela_burton
01159 618 013

Sally Canning
Worksop, Nottinghamshire, England
www.EmoTrance.com/m/sally_canning
01909 472 097

June Eyre
Langley Mill, Nottinghamshire, England
www.EmoTrance.com/m/june_eyre

Maggie Noskeau
Nottingham, Nottinghamshire, England
www.EmoTrance.com/m/maggie_noskeau
0115 9735 807

Belen Sanchez-Arias
North Huskham, Nottinghamshire, England
EmoTrance.com/m/belen_sanchez_arias
01636 672076

England - Oxfordshire

Deborah Labuschagne
Hempton, Oxfordshire, England
EmoTrance.com/m/deborah_labuschagne
07834189579

Lisa Gibbens
Abingdon, Oxon, England
www.EmoTrance.com/m/lisa_gibbens
01235 550454

England - Shropshire

Debra Goldston
Moreton Nr. Newport, Shropshire, England
www.EmoTrance.com/m/debra_goldston
01952 691 542

Katherine Oakley
Shrewsbury, Shropshire, England
EmoTrance.com/m/katherine_oakley

England - Somerset

Marie Andersen
Yeovil, Somerset, England
www.EmoTrance.com/m/marie_andersen
01935 840 256

Lisa Bundfuss
Portishead, Somerset, England
www.EmoTrance.com/m/lisa_bundfuss
01275 844 855

Patricia Moreby
Chilthorne Domer, Somerset, England
www.EmoTrance.com/m/patricia_moreby
01789 841273

Nina Nelson
Charlton Musgrove, Wincanton, Somerset,
England
www.EmoTrance.com/m/nina_nelson
07766 002 752

Jo Russell Smith
Wiveliscombe, Somerset, England
EmoTrance.com/m/jo_russell_smith
01984 623 642

England – South Gloucestershire

Keith Cherrington
Bristol, South Gloucestershire, England
EmoTrance.com/m/keith_cherrington
07900180294

England – South Yorkshire

William Taylor
Sheffield, South Yorkshire, England
www.EmoTrance.com/m/william_taylor

England - Staffordshire

Lindsay Adams
Stafford, Staffordshire, England
www.EmoTrance.com/m/lindsay_adams
07535615617

Deborah Bird
Cannock, Staffordshire, England
www.EmoTrance.com/m/deborah_bird
01543 876612

Helen Dutton
BSc(Hons) CertHP
EmoTrance Practitioner
'Ray of Peace'
Tutbury, Staffordshire.
rayofpeace@hotmail.co.uk
www.rayofpeace.co.uk
07837 642016

Lynn Hyll
Chasetown, Staffordshire, England
www.EmoTrance.com/m/lynn_hyll
07711145516

Andrea Lynam
Cannock, Staffordshire, England
www.EmoTrance.com/m/andrea_lynam
07834 832940

Eileen Strong
Marchington, Staffordshire, England
www.EmoTrance.com/m/eileen_strong
07745 409059

Chris Vurley
Lichfield, Staffordshire, England
www.EmoTrance.com/m/chris_vurley

England - Suffolk

Melanie Bryceland
Bury Saint Edmunds, Suffolk, England
EmoTrance.com/m/melanie_bryceland
07971 075264

England - Surrey

Ken Carmichael
Egham, Surrey, England
www.EmoTrance.com/m/ken_carmichael
07717 850 945

Lesley Labram
Woking, Surrey, England
www.EmoTrance.com/m/lesley_labram
01483 841265

Michelle Lourdes
Lightwater, Surrey, England
EmoTrance.com/m/michelle_lourdes
01276 472 322

Pamela Naidoo
New Malden, Surrey, England
www.EmoTrance.com/m/pamela_naidoo
07944137358

Anne Sweet
East Molesey, Surrey, England

www.EmoTrance.com/m/anne_sweet
02083982455

Kate Towns
Bramley, Surrey, England
www.EmoTrance.com/m/kate_towns
01483 893353

Gabriella Welch
Kingston-Upon-Thames, Surrey, England
www.EmoTrance.com/m/gabriella_welch
07753355446

England - Warwickshire

Carrie Wynne Spencer
Stratford Upon Avon, Warks, England
EmoTrance.com/m/carrie_wynne_spencer
01789 209244

Peter Delves
Kenilworth, Warwickshire, England
www.EmoTrance.com/m/peter_delves
01926 856 746

Helen Dolley
Leamington Spa, Warwickshire, England
www.EmoTrance.com/m/helen_dolley
+44 (0) 7957 708 522

Jilly Parsons
Grendon, Warwickshire, England
www.EmoTrance.com/m/jilly_parsons
01827 898 571

Lilian Poultney
Rugby, Warwickshire, England
www.EmoTrance.com/m/lilian_poultney
01788567033

Paula Turner
Stratford-Upon-Avon, Warwickshire, England
www.EmoTrance.com/m/paula_turner
01789 269378

England – West Midlands

Kiren Bhogal
Solihull, West Midlands, England
www.EmoTrance.com/m/kiren_bhogal
01564 773 980

Nicola G. Day
Wolverhampton, West Midlands, England
www.EmoTrance.com/m/nicola_day
07932664907

Scott Degville
Walsall, West Midlands, England
www.EmoTrance.com/m/scott_degville
07813700978

Lynne Hancher
Wolverhampton, West Midlands, England
www.EmoTrance.com/m/lynne_hancher
01902 850 621

Yvonne Jackson
Birmingham, West Midlands, England
www.EmoTrance.com/m/yvonne_jackson
0121 459 8244

Alexandra Millington
Aldridge, West Midlands, England
EmoTrance.com/m/alexandra_millington
07973 358622

England – West Sussex

Mary Haines
Chichester, West Sussex, England
www.EmoTrance.com/m/mary_haines

Carol Hitchen
Billingshurst, West Sussex, England
www.EmoTrance.com/m/carol_hitchen
01403 783067

Philip Knox
Rudgwick, West Sussex, England
www.EmoTrance.com/m/philip_knox

Sarah Pinkerton
Burgess Hill, West Sussex, England
www.EmoTrance.com/m/sarah_pinkerton
07852105404

Kim Wheeler
Billingshurst, West Sussex, England
www.EmoTrance.com/m/kim_wheeler
01403 783067

England - Wiltshire

Pennie Astbury
Swindon, Wiltshire, England
www.EmoTrance.com/m/pennie_astbury
01793 726 775

England - Yorkshire

Suzanne Kirby
Scarborough, Yorkshire, England
www.EmoTrance.com/m/suzanne_kirby
01527 546173

Karen Tinker
Barnsley, Yorkshire, England
www.EmoTrance.com/m/karen_tinker
01226 380 681

France

Joyce Armini-Rambi
Senlis, France
EmoTrance.com/m/joyce_armini_rambi

Carol Borthwick
Caderousse 84860, Provence, France
www.EmoTrance.com/m/carol_borthwick
0033(0) 561 605 065

Mikael Cormont
Méru, France
www.EmoTrance.com/m/mikael_cormont

Germany

Gitta Berg
Furth-Brombach, Germany
www.EmoTrance.com/m/gitta_berg
+49 (0) 6253 3849, +49 (0) 172 6212984

Stephanie Beyerle
Karlsruhe Fon, Germany
EmoTrance.com/m/stephanie_beyerle
+49 721 - 9767127

Regine Bialojan
Schmitten, Germany
www.EmoTrance.com/m/regine_bialojan
+49 6084 5445

Kurt Brodwolf
Würzburg, Bayern, Germany
www.EmoTrance.com/m/kurt_brodwolf
0049 931285109

Ulrich Goelz
Baden-Wuerttemberg, Germany
www.EmoTrance.com/m/ulrich_goelz
07021 736142

Hilmar Groschupf
Merching, Germany
www.EmoTrance.com/m/helma_groschupf
+49 (0)8233 795980

Petra Groschupf
Merching, Germany
www.EmoTrance.com/m/petra_groschupf
+498233-795980

Margit Heiter
Laupheim, Baden-Württemberg, Germany
www.EmoTrance.com/m/margit_heiter
07392/ 911847

Hella Hergel
Troisdorf, Germany
www.EmoTrance.com/m/hella_hergel
0049 2241 82559

Susanne Hoffmann
Braunschweig, Niedersachsen, Germany
EmoTrance.com/m/susanne_hoffmann
49 531 501913

Werner Jahn
Diesenhofen, Germany
www.EmoTrance.com/m/werner_jahn
89 6283 0330

Josephine Jehmlich
Bayern, Germany
EmoTrance.com/m/josephine_jehmlich
0049 8233 789640

Eva Jetzsperger
Althegnenberg, Germany
www.EmoTrance.com/m/eva_jetzsperger
0049 8202 1034

Irmgard Jäger-Stiehle
Sigmaringen, Baden-Württemberg, Germany
EmoTrance.com/m/irmgard_jger_stiehle
07571/686994

Joerg Kohler
Markdorf, Baden-Wuerttemberg, Germany
www.EmoTrance.com/m/joerg_kohler
+49-7544 742851

Michael Kopp
Baden-Württemberg, Germany
www.EmoTrance.com/m/michael_kopp
0049 (0)8388-920760

Daniela Kuehn
Wesel, Germany
www.EmoTrance.com/m/daniela_kuehn
00492814607472

Renate Kustner
Igersheim, Baden-Württemberg, Germany
www.EmoTrance.com/m/renate_kustner
07931 - 44253

Annette Lunau
Nrw, Germany
www.EmoTrance.com/m/annette_lunau
49 2183 416850

Dieter Mueller
Grossalmerode, Hessen, Germany
www.EmoTrance.com/m/dieter_mueller
+49 5604 5966

EmoTrance Members Directory – Practitioners

Christel Oberreiter
Mulheim An Der Ruhr, Nrw, Germany
EmoTrance.com/m/christel_oberreiter
0208 781315

Antje Ottersdorf
Dummer Ot : Walsmuhlen, Mecklenburg,
Germany
EmoTrance.com/m/antje_ottersdorf
+49 3869 599456

Lutz Rabe
Erbach, Germany
www.EmoTrance.com/m/lutz_rabe
+ 49 6062 956950

Birgitt Reichert
Würzburg, Bayern, Germany
EmoTrance.com/m/birgitt_reichert
0931285109

Birgit Reinert
Stuttgart, Germany
www.EmoTrance.com/m/birgit_reinert
+49 711 632452

Sabrina Rohmer
Burgrieden, Germany
www.EmoTrance.com/m/sabrina_rohmer

Conny Roth
Siegburg, Nrw, Germany
www.EmoTrance.com/m/conny_roth
02241-16-53-66 0

Elisabeth Rüttler
Baden Wurtemberg, Germany
EmoTrance.com/m/elisabeth_rttler
0793144765

Babette Schechtl
Schongeising, Bayern, Germany
EmoTrance.com/m/babette_schechtl
0170 161 3026

Heike Schonert
Hagen, Germany
www.EmoTrance.com/m/heike_schonert
+49 2334 41365 and +49 174 7779935

Anita Schwarzenberg
Propst-Ermward-Ring 62, D-Herzebrock-
Clarholz, Germany
EmoTrance.com/m/anita_schwarzenberg
+49/5245-87000;+49/170-451 34 23

Sonja Seydel
Moenchengladbach, Germany
www.EmoTrance.com/m/sonja_seydel

Margarita Stiehle
Lachen, Bayern, Germany
EmoTrance.com/m/margarita_stiehle
0049-0175 586 1448

Gerald Stiehler
Muehltal, Germany
www.EmoTrance.com/m/gerald_stiehler
+49 (0)6151 520 9478

Detlev Tesch
Bonn, Germany
www.EmoTrance.com/m/detlev_tesch
+49 228 473792

Birgit Ulrich-Reinisch
Leimen, Baden-Württemberg, Germany
EmoTrance.com/m/birgit_ulrich_reinisch1

Susanne Von Grossmann
Meckenheim, Germany
EmoTrance.com/m/susanne_von_grossmann
0049-2225-91630

Kerstin Warkentin
Duesseldorf, Germany
EmoTrance.com/m/kerstin_warkentin
+49 211 432942

Evelyne Wiertelarz
Krautscheid, Rheinland - Pfalz, Germany
EmoTrance.com/m/evelyne_wiertelarz
06554-9009940

Heike Willms-Heib
Germany
EmoTrance.com/m/heike_willms_heib
+49 6581 – 994776

Annelies Winkler
Rudolstadt, Germany
EmoTrance.com/m/annelies_winkler
+49 3672 - 423059

Sabine Witzke
Maintal, Germany
www.EmoTrance.com/m/sabine_witzke
49 0 6109 62420

Iran

Rabea Dehghan
No. 40 Sadaf Building, Tehran, Iran
www.EmoTrance.com/m/rabea_dehghan
0208 810 7346

Ireland

Ruth Bray
Kildorrery, Co Cork, Ireland
www.EmoTrance.com/m/ruth_bray
(+00353) 2 240 913 / 087 7667087

Anna Casey
Dun Laoghaire, Co Dublin, Ireland
www.EmoTrance.com/m/anna_casey
(01) 284 3849

Cliona Farrell
Blackrock,, County Dublin, Ireland
www.EmoTrance.com/m/cliona_farrell
00353 (0)1 2881431

Ray Manning
Dublin 16, Ireland
www.EmoTrance.com/m/ray_manning
00353-1- 298 6507

Ita Mc Tigue
Drumcondra, Dublin, Ireland
www.EmoTrance.com/m/ita_mc_tigue
086 341 4788

Helen McCrarren
Scotstown, Co Monaghan, Ireland
www.EmoTrance.com/m/helen_mccrarren
00353 87412 9385

Paul O'Malley
Dundrum, Dublin, Ireland
www.EmoTrance.com/m/paul_omalley
01 283 2092

Nuala O'Rourke
Goatstown, Dublin, Ireland
www.EmoTrance.com/m/nuala_orourke
00 353 12982 642

Helen Ryle
Tralee, Co Kerry, Ireland
www.EmoTrance.com/m/helen_ryle
00353 87 773 4914

Tom Wynn
Dublin, Dublin, Ireland
www.EmoTrance.com/m/tom_wynn
00353 (1) 868 9596

Israel

Varda Banilivy
Tel Aviv, Israel
www.EmoTrance.com/m/varda_banilivy
+1 516 353 8156

Italy

Fiorenza Yama Bidoli
Milano, Italy
EmoTrance.com/m/fiorenza_yama_bidoli
0039 0289512518

Malaysia

Bernice Leaw
Ampang, Selangor De, Malaysia
www.EmoTrance.com/m/bernice_leaw
+ 6017 337 8819

Northern Ireland

Heather Johnston
Belfast, Co Antrim, N. Ireland
EmoTrance.com/m/heather_johnston
028 90 709 488 or 028 90 792 365

The Netherlands

Shariff Hoesenie
Den Haag, Netherlands
EmoTrance.com/m/shariff_hoesenie
0031-6-26720278

Franklin Sluijters
Ulvenhout, Netherlands
EmoTrance.com/m/franklin_sluijters
+31 76 56 51 468

Joyce Stehmann-Ritter
Zuid-Holland, Netherlands
EmoTrance.com/m/joyce_stehmann_ritter
0031-70-3873513

Lisette Van De Wijgert
Oss, Netherlands
EmoTrance.com/m/lisette_van_de_wijgert
0613096370

Mary Van Der Stam
Geldrop, Netherlands
EmoTrance.com/m/loretta_van_der_stam
+31 40 8428516

Jacolien Van Zutphen
Buren, Gld, Netherlands
EmoTrance.com/m/jacolien_van_zutphen
0344-571370

Margreet Vink
Purmerend, Noordholland, Netherlands
www.EmoTrance.com/m/margreet_vink
0031-299-416444

Norway

Tom Soerevik
Bergen, Norway
www.EmoTrance.com/m/tom_soerevik
+ 4755 168 267

Scotland

Isobel Anderson
Dalkeith, Midlothian, Scotland
www.EmoTrance.com/m/isobel_anderson
01316540690

Nicola Blyth
Edinburgh, Scotland
www.EmoTrance.com/m/nicola_blyth
0131 554 9940

Jackie Cohen
Edinburgh, Scotland
www.EmoTrance.com/m/jackie_cohen
0131 657 1119

Murray Cornish
Newcastleton, Roxburghshire, Scotland
www.EmoTrance.com/m/murray_cornish
01387375736

Morag Foster M.A. PGDE
Dingwall, Ross-Shire, Scotland
EmoTrance.com/m/morag_foster_ma_pgde
01349 865 813

Michele Gamble
Scotland
www.EmoTrance.com/m/michele_gamble
07785971606

Flora Greenhorn
Fauldhouse, West Lothian, Scotland
www.EmoTrance.com/m/flora_greenhorn

Hazel Harris
Blairgowrie, Perthshire, Scotland
www.EmoTrance.com/m/hazel_harris
01250870611

Paula Hogg
Edinburgh, Scotland
www.EmoTrance.com/m/paula_hogg
0131 555 2344

Moyra King
Edinburgh, Scotland
www.EmoTrance.com/m/moyra_king
07818063185

John Macdonald
Edinburgh, Scotland
www.EmoTrance.com/m/john_macdonald

Naomi Mandel
Aberdeen, Aberdeenshire, Scotland
www.EmoTrance.com/m/naomi_mandel
01224 321 110

John Paul Mason
Edinburgh, Scotland
www.EmoTrance.com/m/john_paul_mason
0131 652 1788

Derek Rough
Dunfermline, Fife, Scotland
www.EmoTrance.com/m/derek_rough
01383 881007

Ann Richards
Edinburgh, Scotland
www.EmoTrance.com/m/ann_richards
0131 343 6082

Gordon Soutar
Edinburgh, Midlothian, Scotland
www.EmoTrance.com/m/gordon_soutar
0131 467 0238

Sahajo Southey
Edinburgh, Scotland
www.EmoTrance.com/m/sahajo_southey
07712 760 247

Jo Spaczynska
Edinburgh, Midlothian, Scotland
www.EmoTrance.com/m/jo_spaczynska
0131 556 8878

Duncan Tennant
Livingston, West Lothian, Scotland
www.EmoTrance.com/m/duncan_tennant
01506 438153

Monika Tyrrell
Edinburgh, Scotland
www.EmoTrance.com/m/monika_tyrrell
0131 442 4874

Lorna Veal
Greenock, Scotland
www.EmoTrance.com/m/lorna_veal
01475 634974

Spain

Eilean Drysdale
Jaen, Spain
www.EmoTrance.com/m/eilean_drysdale
0034 953 583 926

Wodnik Miryan
Madrid, Spain
www.EmoTrance.com/m/wodnik_miryan

Sweden

Lise-Lotte Carlsten
Malmö, Sweden
EmoTrance.com/m/lise_lotte_carlsten
+46(0)40 475 542

Susann Forsberg
Löderup, Sweden
www.EmoTrance.com/m/susann_forsberg
+46-(0)709 733 947

Kjell Forsberg
Peppinge (Ystad), Sweden
www.EmoTrance.com/m/kjell_forsberg
+46(0)411527 030

Ann-Sofi Forsberg
Löderup, Sweden
EmoTrance.com/m/ann_sofi_forsberg
+46(0)411 527 030

Rose-Marie Larsson
Billdal, Sweden
EmoTrance.com/m/rose_marie_larsson
46732636488

Peter Lee
Luleå, Sweden
www.EmoTrance.com/m/peter_lee
0920-990 00

EmoTrance Members Directory – Practitioners

Ann-Marie Nilsson
Simrishamn, Sweden
EmoTrance.com/m/ann_marie_nilsson
+46414440 240

Sofia Olsson
Luleå, Sweden
www.EmoTrance.com/m/sofia_olsson
070-325 25 57

Claes Sterner
Alvsjo, Sweden
www.EmoTrance.com/m/claes_sterner
+46 - (0)8- 6494738

Switzerland

Heidi Aegeter
Gurzelen, Bern, Switzerland
www.EmoTrance.com/m/heidi_aegeter
0041 (0) 33 345 5829

Claudia Aeschbach
Basel, Basel-Stadt, Switzerland
EmoTrance.com/m/claudia_aeschbach
0041 79 243 52 77

Rosmarie Ballmer
Muttenz, Basellandschaft, Switzerland
EmoTrance.com/m/rosmarie_ballmer
+41796434704

Werner Baumann
Zurich, Zh, Switzerland
www.EmoTrance.com/m/werner_baumann
0041 44 242 77 74

Ursula Berg
Zug, Switzerland
www.EmoTrance.com/m/ursula_berg
0041 79 207 75 56

Jacqueline Blaser
Liebefeld, Bern, Switzerland
EmoTrance.com/m/jacqueline_blaser
+41 79 377 3215

Christoph Brennenstuhl
Ruti Zh, Zh, Switzerland
EmoTrance.com/m/christoph_brennenstuhl
0041 76 585 8862

Antonio Capuzzi
Biberstein, Aargau, Switzerland
www.EmoTrance.com/m/antonio_capuzzi
0041 793328184

Anne Devecchi
Baden, Aargau, Switzerland
www.EmoTrance.com/m/anne_devecchi
+41 56 222 3009

Stefan Dudas
Wohlen, Switzerland
www.EmoTrance.com/m/stefan_dudas
+41 56 204 94 80

Beatrix Ellenberger Zeller
Neftenbach, Zh, Switzerland
EmoTrance.com/m/beatrix_zeller_ellenberger
0041 52 301 13 47

Adrian Gaal
Kriens, Luzern, Switzerland
www.EmoTrance.com/m/adrian_gaal
+41 41 340 39 39

Vreni Good-Frey
Igis, Graubuenden, Switzerland
www.EmoTrance.com/m/vreni_good_frey
0041 81 322 47 83

Beatrice Hinder
Sankt Gallen, Switzerland
www.EmoTrance.com/m/beatrice_hinder
+41 78 803 33 26

Priska Landis
Pfaeffikon, Schwyz, Switzerland
www.EmoTrance.com/m/priska_landis
+41 79 2323 500

Anita Lang
Riehen, Switzerland
www.EmoTrance.com/m/anita_lang
0041 61 641 17 14

Ursula Luethi
Bern, Switzerland
www.EmoTrance.com/m/ursula_luethi
0041 (0) 33 345 30 50 / 0041 (0) 79 28799 92

EmoTrance Members Directory – Practitioners

Danielle Meier
Ermensee, Luzern, Switzerland
www.EmoTrance.com/m/danielle_meier

Ursula Meister
Grosshoechstetten, Bern, Switzerland
www.EmoTrance.com/m/ursula_meister
+41 31 711 23 14

Markus Meyer
Speicher, Appenzell, Switzerland
www.EmoTrance.com/m/markus_meyer
0713449368

Silvia Müller
Grafenried, Bern, Switzerland
www.EmoTrance.com/m/silvia_mller
0041 31 767 81 07

Brigitte Parpan
Hergiswil, Nidwalden, Switzerland
www.EmoTrance.com/m/brigitte_parpan
0041 416207090

Elisabetta Reist
Lugano, Ticino, Switzerland
EmoTrance.com/m/elisabetta_reist
+4191 911 55 45

Vreni Rueedi
Kriens, Luzern, Switzerland
www.EmoTrance.com/m/vreni_rueedi
0041 41 310 25 43

Heidi Saputelli
Beinwil Am See, Aargau, Switzerland
www.EmoTrance.com/m/heidi_saputelli
062 772 02 34

Richard Scherrer
Luzern, Switzerland
EmoTrance.com/m/richard_scherrer
0041 41 210 22 28

Usula Schmid
Basel, Switzerland
www.EmoTrance.com/m/usula_schmid
061 922 0022

Ursula Schweizer
Aarwangen, BE, Switzerland
EmoTrance.com/m/ursula_schweizer
062 923 5557

Beatrice Thomet
Wabern, Bern, Switzerland
www.EmoTrance.com/m/beatrice_thomet
0041 031 961 5254

Karin Wallimann
Utzenstorf, Switzerland
www.EmoTrance.com/m/karin_wallimann
076 376 80 16

Robert Wilhelmi
Ruggell, Fürstentum Liechtenstein, Switzerland
www.EmoTrance.com/m/robert_wilhelmi
+423 7882 48814

Reto Wyss
Herzogenbuchsee, Berne, Switzerland
www.EmoTrance.com/m/reto_wyss
+41 62 962 9212

Astrid Zapf
Guemligen, Bern, Switzerland
www.EmoTrance.com/m/astrid_zapf

Beatrix Zeller
Berg-Dägerlen, Switzerland
www.EmoTrance.com/m/beatrix_zeller

Ursi Zeller-Schickli
Abtwil, Switzerland
EmoTrance.com/m/ursi_zeller_schickli

Martha Zryd
Norn, Tg, Switzerland
www.EmoTrance.com/m/martha_zryd
071 845 1560

Turkey

Inci Erkin
Alsancak, Izmir, Turkey
www.EmoTrance.com/m/inci_erkin
0090232 422 0365

Ukraine

Svitlana Polyakova
Donetsk, Ukraine
EmoTrance.com/m/svitlana_polyakova

United States

Francine Anderson
Tulsa, Oklahoma, United States
EmoTrance.com/m/francine_anderson

Vincent Bathea
Dallas, Texas, United States
www.EmoTrance.com/m/vincent_bathea
+1 972 824 2079

Jennifer Behrends
New York, United States
EmoTrance.com/m/jennifer_behrends

Lorie Von S Brown
Freeport, New York, United States
EmoTrance.com/m/lorie_von_s_brown
917-445-6886

Abraham Bruck
Monsey, New York, United States
www.EmoTrance.com/m/abraham_bruck
718-687-8805

Diane Cogorno Castro
St.louis, Missouri, United States
EmoTrance.com/m/diane_cogorno_castro
314-726-2584

Gilana Cohn
Yonkers, New York, United States
www.EmoTrance.com/m/gilana_cohn
914-548-3369

Mary Anne Cumbie
Cypress, Texas, United States
EmoTrance.com/m/mary_anne_cumbie

> **Patricia DancingElk**
> **EmoTrance Trainer &**
> **Advanced Practitioner**
> **Texas, United States**
> **972-937-0377**
> **www.EmotranceTexas.com**

Dianna De Groot
Waxahachie, Texas, United States
www.EmoTrance.com/m/dianna_de_groot
(817) 504 1742

Roberta Greene
Willingboro, New Jersey, United States
www.EmoTrance.com/m/roberta_greene
609-346-2132

Susan Grey
Columbia, South Carolina, United States
www.EmoTrance.com/m/susan_grey
803-419-3823

Janette Isaacson
Redmond, Washington, United States
EmoTrance.com/m/janette_isaacson
206-755-6987

Rena Levin
Baltimore, Maryland, United States
www.EmoTrance.com/m/rena_levin
410-913-4057

Jen McFarlane
Kkkk, United States
www.EmoTrance.com/m/jen_mcfarlane

Helen Slomovits
Ann Arbor, Mi, United States
www.EmoTrance.com/m/helen_slomovits
734 665-0409

Carolyn Walker
Dallas, Texas, United States
www.EmoTrance.com/m/carolyn_walker
214-505-6035

Dottie Ward
Morton Grove, Illinois, United States
www.EmoTrance.com/m/dottie_ward
773/972 3789

Wales

Irene Davies
Pontyclun, Mid Glamorgan, Wales
www.EmoTrance.com/m/irene_davies
01443 230700

Ruth Gilmore
Rhoose, Vale Of Glamorgan, Wales
www.EmoTrance.com/m/ruth_gilmore
01446 711464

Alicia Sawaya
Gwalchmai, Isle Of Anglesey, Wales
www.EmoTrance.com/m/alicia_sawaya
01407 720863

Suzi Tarrant
Narberth, Pembrokeshire, Wales
www.EmoTrance.com/m/suzi_tarrant
07941 261037

Lynne Theophanides
Cardiff, Wales
EmoTrance.com/m/lynne_theophanides
02920 259 520

EmoTrance Relationships Consultants

Zeinab Abdel Aziz Alloub
Cairo, Egypt
www.EmoTrance.com/m/zeinab_alloub
+20(0) 10 377 1616

Sahar Fouad Abdel Hay
Cairo, Egypt
EmoTrance.com/m/sahar_fouad_abdel_hay
+20(0) 10 141 9895

Marion Adams
St Albans, Hertfordshire, England
www.EmoTrance.com/m/marion_adams
07532 275339

Khaled Al-Damalawy
Cairo, Egypt
EmoTrance.com/m/khaled_al_damalawy
+20(0)12 219 6392

Mervette Alloub
Cairo, Egypt
www.EmoTrance.com/m/
+20(0) 10 148 7755

Regine Bialojan
Schmitten, Germany
www.EmoTrance.com/m/regine_bialojan
+49 6084 5445

Fiorenza Yama Bidoli
Milano, Italy
EmoTrance.com/m/fiorenza_yama_bidoli
0039 0289512518

Louise Bliss
Northolt, Middlesex, England
www.EmoTrance.com/m/louise_bliss
0208 845 1293 or 07811 447070

Kim Bradley
Hayes, Middlesex, England
www.EmoTrance.com/m/kim_bradley
020 8842 2386 or 07970 584 851

Lisa Bundfuss
Portishead, Somerset, England
www.EmoTrance.com/m/lisa_bundfuss
01275 844 855

Bobbie Carcary
West Malling, Kent, England
www.EmoTrance.com/m/bobbie_carcary
01732 842990

Chris Dawson
EmoTrance Trainer &
Advanced Practitioner
Stockport,Cheshire, UK
Tel: 0161 474 7996
www.stockport-hypnotherapy.co.uk

Dalia El Gebaly
Cairo, Egypt
www.EmoTrance.com/m/dalia_el_gebaly
+20(0)10 657 3365

Khaled El-Sharkawy
Cairo, Egypt
EmoTrance.com/m/khaled_el_sharkawy
+20(0)10 112 8057

Ezzat Ez Aldien
Cairo, Egypt
www.EmoTrance.com/m/ezzat_ez_aldien
+20(0) 12 312 1160

Margarita Foley
London, England
www.EmoTrance.com/m/margarita_foley
020 88019 883

Petra Groschupf
Merching, Germany
www.EmoTrance.com/m/petra_groschupf
+498233-795980

Hilmar Groschupf
Merching, Germany
www.EmoTrance.com/m/helma_groschupf
+49 (0)8233 795980

Hazel Harris
Blairgowrie, Perthshire, Scotland
www.EmoTrance.com/m/hazel_harris
01250870611

Susanne Hoffmann
Braunschweig, Niedersachsen, Germany
EmoTrance.com/m/susanne_hoffmann
49 531 501913

```
┌─────────────────────────────────┐
│         Sandra Hillawi           │
│    EmoTrance Master Trainer,     │
│    Advanced Practitioner and     │
│    author of "The Love Clinic"   │
│  Passion for Health Ltd,  Gosport,│
│         Hampshire, UK            │
│       +44 (0)2392 433 928        │
│  sandra@PassionForHealth.com     │
│      www.SandraHillawi.com       │
└─────────────────────────────────┘
```

Deborah Labuschagne
Hempton, Oxfordshire, England
EmoTrance.com/m/deborah_labuschagne
07834189579

Danielle Meier
Ermensee, Luzern, Switzerland
www.EmoTrance.com/m/danielle_meier

Suzanne Georgina Moody
St Helier, Jersey, England
EmoTrance.com/m/suzanne_georgina_moody
01534 482136

Dieter Mueller
Grossalmerode, Hessen, Germany
www.EmoTrance.com/m/dieter_mueller
+49 5604 5966

Nan Rathjen
Lacey, Washington, United States
www.EmoTrance.com/m/nan_rathjen

Beatrice Salmon-Hawk
Langford, Bedfordshire, England
EmoTrance.com/m/beatrice_salmon_hawk
01462 437350

Heidi Saputelli
Beinwil Am See, Aargau, Switzerland
www.EmoTrance.com/m/heidi_saputelli
062 772 02 34

Alicia Sawaya
Gwalchmai, Isle Of Anglesey, Wales
www.EmoTrance.com/m/alicia_sawaya
01407 720863

Anita Schwarzenberg
Propst-Ermward-Ring 62, D-Herzebrock-Clarholz, Germany
EmoTrance.com/m/anita_schwarzenberg
+49/5245-87000;+49/170-451 34 23

Zena Shubbar
London, England
www.EmoTrance.com/m/zena_shubbar

Kerstin Warkentin
Duesseldorf, Germany
EmoTrance.com/m/kerstin_warkentin
+49 211 432942

Angela Western
Tonbridge, Kent, England
www.EmoTrance.com/m/angela_western
01732 835 477

Robert Wilhelmi
Ruggell, Fürstentum Liechtenstein, Switzerland
www.EmoTrance.com/m/robert_wilhelmi
+423 7882 48814

Beatrix Zeller
Berg-Dägerlen, Switzerland
www.EmoTrance.com/m/beatrix_zeller

EmoTrance Training Materials by DragonRising

DragonRising Publishing is one of the worlds leading personal development specialists and was there at the beginning when Silvia Hartmann formulated her ideas with Nicola Quinn and named their discovery "EmoTrance".

Our website, www.DragonRising.com is visited by many thousands of information seekers each month and our newsletter is the most up-to-date resource for EmoTrance information anywhere. By registering for free on our website you'll also have access to some excellent training materials and product demos.

We are a true 21st century publishing house providing many of our products in electronic versions alongside their postable, physical counterparts.

EmoTrance Books & eBooks

The Official Introduction Guide to EmoTrance

by Various

DragonRising in co-ordination with the custodians of EmoTrance, The Sidereus Foundation have teamed up to produce the EmoTrance 2009 yearbook. This is your perfect introduction guide to this incredible 21st century healing and self-improvement energy technique.

This Paperback is densely packed with information, articles, reviews and includes international practitioner, advanced practitioner & trainer listings.   Contact us for information on our excellent discounts on this title.

The Patterns & Techniques of EmoTrance Trilogy

by Silvia Hartmann

Oceans of Energy: Patterns & Techniques of EmoTrance, vol 1

EmoTrance is a new system for handling the human energy body and thus, radically transforming human emotions and allowing the user to experience new states of bliss, peace and enchantment. This best selling manual provides a thorough grounding in the underlying principles of EmoTrance for self help and healing. It contains all the basic techniques so that the reader can get started

with EmoTrance right away. Highly acclaimed, international best seller, outstanding value.

Living Energy: Patterns & Techniques of EmoTrance, vol 2

Immortality, Thought Flow & Snow Globes, taking control of the Autogenic Universe, The Energy Of Learning, Heart Healing and the human energy body Super Systems are just some of the many topics and techniques covered in this exciting manual which continues the research and journey into the Living Universe. Fascinating, radical, and very different, EmoTrance Vol. 2, Living Energy invites us to change our lives through changing the energetic realities we create in our lives today.

Energy Magic: Patterns & Techniques of EmoTrance, vol 3

Working with the existing energetic realities behind the constructs of human lives directly has always been held to be magic, secret knowledge known only by the privileged few. Energy Magic takes reality creation through word, thought, movement and symbol finally out of the dark ages and makes Energy Magic accessible to everyone - and easily so. A splendid and truly magical book that cannot help but educate, inspire and transform the ideas of what we can do, and how to do it.

EmoTrance BeautyT: The Book

by Silvia Hartmann

Follow with this fascinating journey as Dr Hartmann builds a different body image from the ground up, step by step as this extraordinary training unfolds. A unique and profound healing of the oldest wounds of all, and a priceless gift to practitioners and clients with the power to change lives and destinies in single session. This book contains a full transcript and all the original exercises and lectures from the BeauTy T training.

The Love Clinic

by Sandra Hillawi

In the Love Clinic, Energy Expert Sandra Hillawi reveals the real reasons for the problems with love and relationships, and explains in accessible, every day language, what we can do to alleviate problems and pain, and to start experiencing the joy of love in a whole new way.

Using the latest techniques available in energy research to date, and based on the experience of thousands of people who have successfully used these new methods to rid themselves of love pain, jealousy, low self esteem and negative emotions in relationships, Sandra Hillawi shows us that it is easy to love - if you know how.

Supported with many real case stories and detailed descriptions and instructions, The Love Clinic is a practical, engaging book that wll be of interest to anyone who wants to improve their experience with loving, and being loved.

The Enchanted World

by Silvia Hartmann

UK researcher Dr Silvia Hartmann, creator of Project Sanctuary, The Harmony Program and EmoTrance has written this book especially as an introduction to the presuppositions of her life's work. 65 Super Concise Chapters to lay down the step stones for anyone to enter "The Enchanted World" - the one true Universe that sings and dances with life, and love of life. Easy to read, multilevel depth of information that speaks to the reader in a very personal fashion. Highly Recommended.

EmoTrance Recorded Materials

The First Introduction to EmoTrance Oxford 2002

by Silvia Hartmann

This is a live 90 minute historical recording of Silvia Hartmann presenting the first ever EmoTrance lecture to the participants of the 2002 Oxford Energy Therapy conference. Now we are four years on, EmoTrance has become a truly global phenomenon and we have decided to make this rare recording available in CD or MP3. This lecture gives you the perfect opportunity to understand EmoTrance from its developmental roots and history to its concepts and protocols. This recording also includes audience examples, questions and demonstrations.

The Gatwick 2006 Recordings

with Silvia Hartmann, Nicola Quinn & Sandra Hillawi

EmoTrance Personal Experience Day Live Recordings

On the 28th April 2006, EmoTrance co-developer Nicola Quinn presented the brand new EmoTrance Self-Help Experience Day syllabus for the first time at London Gatwick UK. This is your opportunity to purchase the complete edited audio recordings that where made that day, together with the comprehensive EmoTrance Self-Help Experience day workshop training manual.

EmoTrance Complete Practitioner Training Live Recordings

In April 2006, EmoTrance Dr Silvia Hartmann, PhD presented the brand new EmoTrance Practitioner syllabus for the first time at London Gatwick UK. This is your opportunity to purchase the complete edited audio recordings of the self help and practitioner workshops. Offer includes the new & revised comprehensive Official EmoTrance Practitioner manual

EmoTrance BeauTy T Professional

with Silvia Hartmann

For professionals, this live training recording contains all you need to get started with offering BeauTy T treatments to your clients. This unique and exclusive set of 4 Audio CDs includes the complete range of hypnotic energy learning, examples, explanations and exercises of the BeauTy T Training. Included as a special  bonus, CD 5 is a Home Self Help BeautyT treatment, and the BeauTy T book. Also available in MP3 & PDF download format.

EmoTrance Self-Help CDs

EmoTrance Energy Dancing

by Silvia Hartmann

NEW - Experience a totally new and exciting way to heal your energy body, exercise your physical body and delight your mind and soul - all at the same time with the revolutionary EmoTrance Energy Dancing. A full and comprehensive Energy Dancing program taught by Dr Silvia Hartmann - Fabulous Stress Buster, Motivator, Re-Energizer and Energy Healer for all ages and all levels of fitness.

EmoTrance Soften & Flow Energy Hypnosis Session

by Silvia Hartmann & Ananga Sivyer

Silvia Hartmann, Creator of EmoTrance, and Ananga Sivyer, Creator of Sonic Solutions, have combined their best energies, instructions and skills to assist YOU in "softening and flowing away" energetic injuries and emotional pain. Just 15 minutes to release, relaxation and a real clearing of the energy system - fast, effective and most of all, it feels great. To enjoy this program and benefit from it, you do not have to know EmoTrance as this Energy Hypnosis product simply takes you where you need to go.

EmoTrance Distance Learning

Certified EmoTrance Practitioner Online Course

Become a fully certified practitioner of EmoTrance with this superb and exciting online distance learning course.

Full to the brim with delightful information and with wonderful, challenging and immensely rewarding exercises especially designed for the distance learning student by Dr Silvia Hartmann, Creator of EmoTrance, this course will not just bring new ideas, skills, knowledge, techniques and abilities, but also the confidence to work with others and help them feel joy when there was only pain and suffering.

A fantastic online course in 8 Units, leading to full certification as a Practitioner of EmoTrance, with experienced tutor support throughout that will transform the beginner and supercharge the experienced energy worker.

Contact DragonRising

Stay in touch with DragonRising by registering on our site www.DragonRising.com and gain access to all our free downloads.

Address:

DragonRising Publishing
The StarFields Network Ltd
Compass House, 45 Gildredge Road
Eastbourne, East Sussex, BN21 4RY
United Kingdom

Phone:

01323 700 123 (United Kingdom)
646 496 9857 (US + Canada)
0044 1323 700 123 (International)

Website:

www.DragonRising.com

Contact Us Online:

www.DragonRising.com/contact

EmoTrance Recommends...

EmoTrance Recommends...

PASSION for HEALTH

Sandra Hillawi is a Master Trainer of EmoTrance and trained with Silvia Hartmann at the launch in 2002.

Since then Sandra has given 100s of EmoTrance training events, training 100s of practitioners in the UK and internationally and is a regular presenter at the annual EmoTrance conference. She is also an experienced MET/EFT Trainer with the AMT and author of best selling book on Relationships, The Love Clinic.

With her office in Gosport, Hampshire UK, Sandra offers :

- **Private consultations internationally** by telephone, or in person in Gosport
- **EmoTrance Training** at Introductory, Advanced and Trainer levels
- **International Workshops** in the UK, Europe, USA, Egypt

For all training dates visit the websites or contact Sandra directly.

Email : Sandra@passionforhealth.com

Tel : +44 (0)2392 433928   Skype : sandrahillawi

Websites : www.passionforhealth.com www.sandrahillawi.com www.youtube.com/sandrahillawi

---

EmoTrance Texas

- Be amazed at how good you can feel.
- Gain new skills to enhance your current healing practice as a therapist, professional healer, counselor, or health care worker.
- Trance-form old emotional burdens without the pain of talking about or re-experiencing the trauma.
- Enhance your current relationships. Issues can be worked out simple, quick and painless.

Patricia DancingElk, EmoTrance Practitioner/Trainer, 214-478-6703
Carolyn Walker, EmoTrance Practitioner, 214-320-1698
www.EmoTranceTexas.com

www.TheAMT.com

The AMT *Online*

Welcome To A New World Of Healing!

The official website of the Association for Meridian Energy Therapies (The AMT)

- Stay in touch with the very latest news and events
- Free downloads and essays
- Mailing lists
- Book Reviews & Product Reviews
- Stay up-to-date with the latest techniques and innovations of the field
- Find a certified AMT Meridian Therapist near you
- Many fully searchable and interesting articles written by leaders of the field.

Simply logon to http://TheAMT.com and start browsing!

Tapping Into Unlimited Creativity Has Never Been This Easy...

EmoTrance is the most advanced technique for working with the Human Energy Body and Project Sanctuary is the most advanced technique for working with the Human Energy Mind.

In 2008, the Project Sanctuary process became even easier and far more accessible after Dr Silvia Hartmann launched The Genius Symbols which are 23 symbols that can change your life!

Discover The Genius Symbols today, visit:

www.DragonRising.com

"If you can type, you can have your own website!"

SpaceNode is a new innovation in website technology which gives you all the benefits of owning your own professional website whilst also being a part of the social networking revolution pioneered by sites such as Facebook, MySpace and Twitter.

Have you ever:

 Bought yourself a website or spent hours making your own, yet become disappointed by the lack of traffic to your site?

 Spent hours on social networking, yet wished you could update your own site just as easily so your content stays on your site?

 Got stuck with a site that is hard to update and keep fresh?

 Wanted your first own professional website (eg: www.yourdomain.com) and email address (eg: yourname@yourdomain.com) for handing out to clients?

 Got sick of the amount of spam you receive, or lost access to your email address when you changed broadband suppliers?

 Wanted to move your existing website to someone who cares?

SpaceNode is the solution for you and has been designed to be the perfect remedy for these 21st century problems. By combining a clever mix of content management website software, with the true benefits of social networking, we have created software that is powerful, easy to use and keeps you and your message in contact with the world.

SpaceNode loves EmoTrance AND the hard working people who promote it. We want you to be proud of your web presence, so we've created an extra special introductory offer for EmoTrance people where you get 12 months for the price of 6 on any of our packages ranging from £4.97 to £19.97 per month. That's a saving of up to £119.82 on your first year!

To find out more about SpaceNode, this offer and the endless possibilities, please visit:

http://SpaceNode.com/emotrance-offer.htm

EmoTrance Recommends...

STRESSED OUT?

Let The StressFish Help!

Stress Tips
Laughter & Stress
Nature Cures
Outside
Quick De-Stress
Stress Info
Anti-Stress Methods
Anti-Stress Books & CDs
The StressFish Blog

Visit www.StressFish.com - ALL WELCOME!

Now YOU Can Study To Be A REAL
EmoTrance Practitioner
in the comfort of your own home.

**Discover the JOY of EmoTrance
for your self, your loved ones
and your clients!**

Help people lead a happier life -
Become An EmoTrance Practitioner.

Easy, Affordable - And Simply Wonderful.

The Official EmoTrance Distance Learning Program with full tutor support:

www.EmoTrance.com

The EmoTrance Conference

New Directions In EmoTrance

- **The Seventh Annual International EmoTrance Conference**
- **At The Europa Hotel, Gatwick, United Kingdom**
- **Conference 25th-26th April 2009**
- **Pre-Conference Fast Track Practitioner Day 24th April 2009**
- **Post-Conference EmoTrance Trainers Day 27th April 2009**

In 2009 the EmoTrance Conference returns for a seventh time bigger and better than ever! Just like the excellent 2008 conference, attendence is only open to Practitioners of EmoTrance, Advanced Practitioners, and of course, EmoTrance Trainers ONLY.

The New Format Annual Conference represents a wonderful opportunity for you:

- To renew friendships and meet with other EmoTrance practitioners and trainers;

- To work with NEW materials & techniques from the professional viewpoint;

- To use the support from other EXPERIENCED practitioners;

- To find out how the latest developments and NEW techniques can benefit YOU;

- To advance your career as an EmoTrance practitioner or trainer.

Practitioners & Above ONLY

With the doors closed to the general public, we can get to work straight away – no more time is lost in explaining the basics, these are two days of intensive, fabulous, in-depth, advanced EmoTrance at its best.

Take Home the Best of the Latest Techniques

Designed from the ground up for practitioners and above, all the new techniques and exercises are not just experienced, but also taught so that they can be taken home and used by the participants to delight their existing clients, as well as open up new opportunities for bringing the joy of EmoTrance to many more people all around the world.

Outstanding Benefits & Bonus for the Participants

Amongst the many benefits and bonuses for the participants are automatic accreditation as an Advanced Practitioner by virtue of conference attendance; a comprehensive conference manual that contains the "How To" of the new techniques, step by step; the trainer's buffet and networking party; and the chance to meet with and work with the most experienced EmoTrance creators, researchers and trainers on the planet today in a friendly and mutually supportive atmosphere.

Pre and Post Conference Trainings

This year, a fast track practitioner training will be offered on the Friday to allow sincerely interested parties to join in with the conference which begins on Saturday. On Monday, the truly amazing NEW Trainer's Day is offered – become a qualified EmoTrance trainer, and work with existing EmoTrance trainers on a peer basis to help each one of us become a star.

Featuring presentations by Dr Silvia Hartmann, Creator of EmoTrance, Master Trainer Sandra Hillawi, and many other experienced EmoTrance Trainers, the NEW conference format is a wonderful opportunity to connect with others who love "the spirit of EmoTrance" and take this fabulous energy modality to the next level.

For booking information and full program, please see:

http://EmoTrance.com/

See You There ...!